Dear Virginia

By Arden Ray Wolfe

A true crime story of ferocious American white privilege – murder without consequences: the incredible victory of a Cherokee American Indian girl adopted for persecution, sexual abuse, and profit.

Not for the faint of heart.

Edited by Artemis Bullwark and Shaun M Jooste

CONTENTS

Dedication

I dedicate this book to Tori, Lisa Fay, and Pamela

Thank you for your friendship, love, support, and humor, which I cherish every day. I couldn't have written this book without you three.

The following letter is to the State of Virginia Department of Social Services, solely responsible for the lack of vetting in my 1967 adoption.

Dear Virginia

Prologue

Dear Virginia,

You failed me miserably. And all because you saw something shiny and not the darkness that lurked just below the surface. No, you saw on adoption papers (because you didn't actually meet him) an attorney with a law degree from Georgetown University, a housewife, and their seventeen-month-old son that they privately adopted the day after his birth. Virginia, you only saw what you wanted to see back in 1967. You clearly did not do even a simple background check on these two people because if you had, you would have realized you were literally handing this half-blooded Cherokee baby girl over to the wolves.

I am going to start with what happened when I was seventeen years old. An event that could have changed my entire future.

It was 1984. I was in the bathroom getting ready for school when the door swung open and slammed against the bathroom wall with a loud BANG! I should have been used to that kind of entrance from my mother, but I never was. I had on a new red skort (skirt with shorts underneath) that I had bought with my own money from my job at a local restaurant. My mother immediately began slapping me hard on my face and punching me in my stomach. It could be she hated that I could buy clothing of my own. She grabbed me by my hair and pulled it really hard. When she let go of my hair, something in me finally.... Snapped!

Years of her violence. Years of horrible and despicable abuse to me. Years of daily beatings and kicking me so hard on my shins with her cowboy boots and leaving continuous black and blue bruises from my knees to my ankles. Years of her fingernails on my ribs and down my back. Years of swollen and black eyes. Years of bruises on my neck and my cheeks. Years of never fighting back. Years of being called a "fucking little cunt." Years that I didn't have a mother's protection. Years of fear…until that very moment.

I had years of deep rage that had simmered and finally EXPLODED to the surface. The next thing I knew, I had both of my hands around her neck. The complete shock on my mother's face made me squeeze harder, and keep squeezing. I had never felt that power before. For the first time in my life, I saw fear in my mother's eyes and... I enjoyed it.

So many years of being told I was "ugly and stupid." I kept on squeezing harder. Years of internal rage at the physical, verbal, and mental abuse I suffered daily had finally burst, and even at that moment, I didn't know how deep it truly ran. My uncontrollable anger resulted in violent action, and at the same time, I was so calm inside. I was choking my abuser and looking straight into her cruel, scared eyes.

I do not know how long I stood there with my hands around her neck. It was as if I drifted off to another place. A place of calm and no noise. A place I could breathe. I don't know how long that lasted. Then I saw something, call it a vision, come into my dreamlike view.

I was behind bars, in a prison cell all alone, and no one cared why I was pushed into killing my mother.

Then it happened. I felt a light tap on my left shoulder, and I heard my name spoken with such clarity and with a softness. I later learned that this was my angel of protection.

I would learn years later in therapy that I was in a disassociated state because when I came too, I was still choking my mother. Her face was a flushed red. Her eyes were watery and filled with utter fear and panic. I let go of her throat, and she fell to the ground on her hands and knees. I stood over her, listening to her gasp for air, choking and coughing. I felt powerful. I had no remorse for the pain she was in. As I walked out of the bathroom, in a very calm and deep tone, I simply said, "If you ever touch me again, I WILL kill you." Then I walked out of the house and went to school.

Yes, Virginia, you failed me miserably because you didn't do your due diligence, and I paid a huge price for that.

☐

Earliest Memories - 1970 - the hell that would become my life

One of my earliest memories: I was three years old and happily jumping off our private dock and swimming around in the lake. My parents had a lake house in Virginia Beach, Virginia. We lived in Richmond in a white two-story house in a cul de sac the rest of the time. The cabin on the lake was a maroon color with a dark green trim. The back porch was off the kitchen and completely screened in to keep the bugs out. The house sat higher than the dock and was only a few feet away. My paternal adoptive grandmother was sitting on a chair with her cane in hand, at the house-end of the dock watching me, staying out of range of me and my splashing. My mother was not there. I don't know where she was. I was a happy little three-year-old having fun in the water.

I was told by an Aunt that I loved the water and took to it before I was even two years old. It shocked my Aunt many years later that my description of both houses was so accurate.

I was swimming around and having a nice time, but then my father suddenly appeared. He swam up to me while I was treading water. While looking at my grandmother, my father gave me instructions to play a joke on my grandmother. He told me to go jump off the dock, then pretend I was drowning, and he would save me. I still remember the feeling of not feeling right about doing that, but he got me to do it anyway.

I jumped off the dock and swam a little way, then I pretended to drown. My father swam over as if he was saving me and, he told me to wave and laugh to let grandmother know it was a joke. But my grandmother had rushed to the end of the dock with her cane, thinking I really was in trouble. My father grabbed me and swam to the dock. He then yanked me out of the water and spanked me hard in front of her. I was wet, and he had pulled my suit down, spanking me so hard my little butt was red. I cried so loud in pain, and I was so confused by what just happened. That is when my Grandmother told me I was a horrible little girl for pulling such a stunt. I told her that father told me to do it. In an angry voice, he told me to stop lying.

It would take lots of therapy to see that this was my adoptive father's master manipulation at work, and it was a regular theme in my young life. This was also the beginning of me being afraid of my Grandmother because she was mean to me from that day on. Mean with her words and actions. She never touched me, but I was afraid of the cane she always carried. I was clearly the "adopted" one, and she treated me awfully from then on.

Now, I'm not sure when the next event happened. I was the same age, so it was probably the same summer. Again, we were at the lake house, and neither my mother nor my brother was around. It was my father who took me to the beach nearby. There were coals from a recent beach campfire still burning bright red. My father held me by my wrists, letting my feet dangle over the coals. He did this several times while I cried out, and he laughed. Then he dropped me into the middle of the coals, so I had to go across them to get away from him!

I don't remember going back to the cabin. I only remember crying and my mother taking me to the doctor.

Hours later, I would hear my parents yelling at each

other about me. I would find out that I was drugged up for the severe blisters on my feet that he caused. That incident, those drugs, opened the door further to my misery and abuse, and the constant mind fuck. They never expected me to remember anything that was done to me.

Yes, Virginia, you failed me. If you had just done a simple background check, there is no way you would have placed me in the hell that would become my life.

It was 1970. That same year, my parents would sell both homes; my father sold my mother's treasured TR3 British green convertible and then bought a motorhome. It was her idea to sell the homes and buy the motorhome as an attempt to start over and get away from her husband's large family. I know this because of their arguments over the years. She was angry at him for selling her car. She had found out she was three months pregnant and wanted a fresh start three thousand miles away in the Pacific wonderland known as Portland, Oregon.

I have a lot of memories from when we lived in Virginia, but I only have one vague memory of that trip three thousand miles across country. I can't tell you how long it took and if we visited any sites. That vague memory? It was in Las Vegas; a strange man handed my father money inside our motorhome, and then my father left me there crying with that strange man.

I don't remember exactly when we arrived in Portland, Oregon. I just remember that I was in a strange, cold room with men who came and went. I remember wishing I was a boy so strange men would stop hurting me.

There is one memory of me in preschool. I don't remember what I did, but the teacher told my mother that something wasn't right. Because of that, I didn't go back to that school. In fact, I believe that this was the beginning of moving me around when questions would arise.

When I was five years old, we moved to the Multnomah Hills area on SW Troy Street in Portland. It was a two-story house with a detached garage on the right side set back a little bit and the driveway in front of it. There was a little front yard with a brick walkway leading to the two-step front porch that had two columns, one on each side. With the front door open, you could see that there was a wood floor inside with the stairs leading up to the bedrooms.

Downstairs, to the left of the stairs, was the living room,

to the right was the dining room, and the kitchen was off of that. All the rooms downstairs were connected, like a circle. Off the kitchen was the back door to the backyard with the entrance to the basement. There were three huge pine trees that lined up along the fence with the neighbor to the left. The backyard was a good size. There were no neighbors to the right but, there was a dirt driveway that led behind our house to another house. Next to that driveway was a two-story square cement building with a fence around it, topped with barbwire. I want to say it was a Pacific Bell building. This house on SW Troy Street would be where I would find out I was adopted and why but, I will come back to that later.

By now, Virginia, you're probably thinking what happened to me is rare, but I am a human being, Virginia. I count. I matter.

I remember my mother walking up the stairs to the bedrooms with me behind her. At the top of the stairs on the left side was what would be my bedroom. I watched my mother's face as I got to the top and looked into my bedroom. I went to the other side of her to see what she was looking at. My father was placing the last square of the pink and white shag carpet. He pulled a square out of the box, peeled the paper off, then sprayed the back of the square and fit it in like a puzzle piece.

In actuality, I'd come to learn that he hired someone to do most of the work and took credit for doing it. A habit he had his entire life.

I stood there in the doorway, taking in this bedroom. The carpet was pink and white shag. The twin bed had a white lace bedspread sprinkled with tiny pink flowers. There was a canopy above the bed that matched the bedspread on a pretty white frame. The dressers were both white, and there was a large white hutch with three shelves and two cabinets underneath that stood by a window.

On those shelves were very fancy dolls dressed up in dresses representing different countries. By the other window was a small table and a white toy box with pink flowers. I didn't recognize anything. I clearly remember my father turning to look at me with a fake smile and fake voice saying, "This is your room." At five years old, I already knew when he was lying. I remember shaking in fear. I looked over to my mother, who appeared angrier than normal.

Sometime after we moved into that house, I remember sitting in the living room wearing dark blue GARANIMAL© corduroy pants with a white button-down round collar shirt. I remember the outfit because the clothes had tags of cartoon animals on them, and to put outfits together, you match the tags. They were in the clothing section of the nearby Fred Meyers store. I also remember them because, in the dressing room, my mother got angry with me and dug her long fingernails into my side until she hurt me. I cried out; someone asked if everything was ok from the other side of the curtain in the dressing room.

One day, in the living room, our black lab Pokey was next to me while my father was reading something when my mother walked through on her way to the kitchen and said angrily, "For Christ's sake Bill, tell the child where she came from!"

The clothes I was wearing indicate that I was attending the catholic school kindergarten not far away next to the catholic church. I must have had questions at school. So my father started by talking about a bunch of babies in a baby store and how he personally picked me out.

From the kitchen, I could hear my mother screaming, and she came back to the living room and said, "Are you fucking kidding me Bill?!"

"Tell her the truth, or I will."

I already knew he was lying because of his voice. My mother stared at me. I remember the fear I felt at five years old, but I knew she would never beat me in front of my father. Then she told me this, "Your biological mother was a 22-year-old teacher who wanted absolutely nothing to do with you. You are a bastard child." The reality is my mother was right.

I would find out years later that my biological mother's name was Alice, that she was Cherokee Indian and a teacher in Manassas, Virginia, where I was born. But she wasn't 22, she was 31. I was the product of an affair. She hid her pregnancy, never seeing a doctor until her water broke when she walked into Prince William Hospital on a Tuesday morning. She never held me or wanted to know that I was a girl. Alice walked out of the hospital later that day and returned to her job the following morning. After meeting her once many years later, I know that to this day she has never told anyone that I exist.

I remember sitting there with fear and then asked this question, "But wasn't my brother adopted too?" This made her fly off the handle.

I guess I should expand a little on that brother, Nick. But, you already know that Virginia because it would have been in the paperwork. He was adopted the day after his birth owing to the fact that my father had connections as an attorney. I use the term "brother" lightly.

He was seventeen months older than me. My first memory of him? We were in the Richmond, Virginia, house on the couch watching Godzilla in black and white on the tv. My brother had a book in his hand. I must have been asking him something. His answer was to hit me so hard sideways with the corner of his book that it cut my eyeball! My mother took me to the doctor where I left with an eyepatch. I still remember the little corduroy jacket with the three leather buttons I was wearing. I remember how I would rub those buttons when I got scared.

I can't tell you what his favorite color was or even his favorite author. I can't tell you much of anything because I was so isolated from the rest of the "family." As a child growing up, I could never understand why I was adopted and yet hated so much. But Nick was spoiled rotten, and he punched me whenever he felt like it. It was so bad that every day my cruel, sadistic mother called me horrible names, kicked and punched me. Her typical rage thing was to pull me by my hair from room to room. If the dog hadn't been let outside to poop by the back door, my five-year-old face would be shoved into the poop!

Then I was screamed at to clean it up, before I was even allowed to clean up my face! My mother beat me so badly one day the neighbor next door called the police. I was in the closet under the stairs, my nose bleeding, and I was cowering in the corner behind boxes - too scared to come out. I don't remember much of the rest of the day after that.

Virginia, even when I did the simplest background check, I found that my father's law partner was the one who almost adopted my brother. I also found out that his former law partner wanted nothing to do with Bill shortly after that adoption. In fact, his law partner wouldn't even talk to me, but his lovely wife did years later when I had questions. Keep reading Virginia, because you need to see <u>how horribly you failed</u>.

There was a knock at our front door. My brother was out playing with friends, and my father wasn't around. I heard my mother talking to someone, so I snuck out of my room to peek. It was easy to peek because my room was at the top of the stairs. My mother's back was to me with the door open, her arm stretched out, holding it as she stood talking to a woman.

Clearly my mother was not letting this woman in. As I stood there, I heard my mother say, "Oh she's not here." Then the woman looked past my mother, up at me, and smiled.

"There she is," she gently said. My mother turned around slowly, giving me her glare that sent me shaking immediately.

"Well, she doesn't have a swimsuit anyway," my mother informed her.

With that the woman kept smiling and said, "That's okay; we have plenty."

That woman was the mother of my brother's friend. The friend came from a big family that had an above-ground square swimming pool in their backyard. The woman held her hand out, and I came running down the stairs. Imagine that? I had never met this woman, yet I ran to her. Off we went the two blocks to her house.

When we got there she gave me a few choices of suits to wear. I picked one out, and then she gave me privacy to change. When I came out, she smiled sweetly, her eyes changing into sympathy, but she tried to keep her sweet smile. She could see clearly that I had been beaten with a belt on the back and front of my legs. There were fingernail scratches all over my body, along with all the bruises up and down my shins. She held my chin in her hand, and told me in a lovely, kind voice to go have fun with the other kids. That was the best day of my five-year-old life!

That wonderful, kind woman must have reported the abuse because I was taken to another house, but my brother wasn't. I don't know how long I was away. When I came back, they put me in the public school at Multnomah Elementary. I would finish kindergarten there, but not before my teacher called my mother in for a conference.

She was told that I was a very well-behaved child but feared I couldn't read since I would never read out loud. She asked if anything had happened to me. I didn't understand that question at the time. My mother had a way of acting like a caring mother with a troubled adopted child. That would be the beginning of me listening to my parents telling anyone concerned about me that I was adopted, that I lied all time, and how troubling that was to them, my parents. This of course was to cover up the reality of what they were doing to me.

As for my reading skills? My mother pulled a magazine from my teacher's desk and slapped it down in front of me and said, " READ!" I did because she scared me. I had learned to read at a young age before I even started school.

It would be over 40 years before I would learn that the houses they owned were in different counties. There was the house in Portland, the farmhouse in Woodburn, and the lake house on Devil's Lake in Lincoln City. They were not that far away from each other, purposely in different counties. I would realize this years later.

My memories have lots of blanks between the ages of five and eight, and yet there are some very detailed ones. It's no wonder. With therapy, I learned it was a way for my brain to protect me from what I would eventually discover about my tortured youth.

I was around six years old at the Troy St. house. My father dressed me in a pretty dress to go to church. That was another thing. There were dresses in my closet that I could wear and fancy dresses I was never allowed to even touch. He had a way of controlling me through manipulation. One way was to have a big smile, tell me that mommy was mean; then he would take me for ice cream.

On that particular day, he took me to our church for what would be my first attendance at a funeral. I had no idea what was going on. I excused myself to go to the bathroom. On the way back, I passed a coffin. I stopped because I didn't know what it was. There was a man in there, dressed in a suit. He looked at me and sat up. He was holding a rosary. He looked kind of familiar, but I don't know who he was.

I was not scared. I'm not really sure how long we talked. Then, a bright light appeared in front of me. Not near him, but in front of me. It was gone within a few seconds. The man was laying back down when a group of people opened the doors and walked in. One woman asked me in a sweet tone what I was doing and if I was lost? I began explaining what happened. That's when my father walked in. Somehow, the adults stopped, looked at me, and then looked at him. That's when my father did his fake laugh and asked what was going on. As a child, I didn't understand the heaviness of the room. Thats when my father started his line he would use my entire life, and I quote: "She likes to tell little stories."

I will never forget the look between my parents when I would bring that situation up years later. Somehow, the story turned into me having a conversation with a man who was my father's client and how weird I was as a child.

After the service, we drove around while he made me drink Squirt soda. Squirt Soda always made me sleepy as a child. I vaguely remember him carrying me into the house. Anytime he gave me a drink, there probably was one of my mother's sedatives in it. Now, this next situation would haunt me for years.

I remember strange men and money being exchanged. I remember a camera. I remember my pretty dress. Then I remember my mother screaming and stuff being thrown, but I was too sleepy. I remember when I woke up, I saw snakes EVERYWHERE. Along my canopy, my dressers, my cabinets, and in the shag carpet. I screamed and screamed before both parents came running in, angry with me. Then I saw snakes all over him, the man that was supposed to be my father! I pointed at him, and out of my mouth came, "You are a very bad man."

The next memory I had was waking up at our lake house in Lincoln City; my mother and brother weren't there. I was in a tee shirt and underwear, so I put on a pair of tiny jeans and a sweatshirt. The next thing I remember was that we were at *The Pixie Kitchen.* I was crying in the bathroom when some waitresses came in trying to console me. They were so kind. I distinctly remember him coming into the bathroom to get me. When they tried to protect me by putting themselves in front of me, he pushed past them. As usual, he got his way.

Now Virginia, if you haven't figured it out, this poor excuse for a man, this sexual predator, was able to abuse me by waving his stature as an attorney with a Georgetown law degree in front of any obstacles to his desires. Well, this was Oregon in the 1970s, and he ALWAYS got his way.

Changes

I'm not sure how long we were in Lincoln City, but when we returned to the Troy St. house, everything in my room was gone, including my clothes. I was only allowed to wear boys' clothes, and my mother chopped my hair so short; I was mistaken as a boy.

There was only my bed with a large blanket on it and the little table in the corner. Even the molding for the canopy was gone. There wasn't even a pillow for my head. I walked over to the table, sat in the one chair. Now, there's a funny thing in our culture about invisible playmates. Children never question where they come from. I can't give you details of what these three women looked like or their names. But I can tell you they were there to play with me, teach me little things, and most of all, comfort me at night. I cried every night. They would surround me and sing softly until I fell asleep.

One night, my door opened, and there my father stood at the doorway. I sat up in fear, and that's when it happened. One of the ladies got up, held her arms as to block him from coming in, and then she screamed.....NOOOOO! The scream didn't hurt my ears at all. I will never forget the look on his face and my voice saying to him, "They don't want you in here." He turned around and left, slamming my door shut.

First Grade

I started first grade at Multnomah Elementary. The main building was for the big kids, and the little kids were in the separate buildings below and to the side, separated by a playground. On the first day of school, I found my desk with my name on it. When class began, our teacher read off our names one by one. To her credit, she is only one of two teachers throughout my childhood who did not mispronounce my name. (I use the name Arden because that was the name on my adoption papers and for my own protection.) In a nice tone, she said what a beautiful name I had, (and it is), but did I have a nickname? I didn't know what a nickname was and must have had a puzzled look on my face. She explained what a nickname was, something short, maybe something my mother called me.

I told her in a soft voice, while looking down at my

desk, "She calls me fucking little cunt." By the look on my teacher's face, I knew she wasn't mad at me, but as an adult, I now realize what it was. It was shock. She didn't want to scare or upset me. I felt shame on that day.

My mother was called in after school. I sat in fear. I was in complete fear of my mother as she tried to explain that I was "nothing but a liar." That "every word out of my mouth was a lie." I sat there physically shaking in my little chair next to my teacher as she let my mother go on. Of course, my mother acted like the concerned mother, until my teacher called her bluff. I mean, called her bluff outright. She told my mother there was no way a child my age would make up such a horrible thing. That the word used clearly came from an adult.

That's when my mother's attitude changed from the caring and concerned mother, to the glare. She literally yanked me out of my chair and, as we were leaving, threatened my teacher that she would be sued if she spread lies about her. When we got home, my mother beat me, kicked me, pulled me by my hair all around the first floor, and dragged me up the stairs to my room, where she kicked me from my door to the window. With every kick, she screamed at me with only curse words and horrible names. She only stopped because she was tired and out of breath.

I lay there in a ball, crying with my nose bleeding. I must have sobbed myself to sleep because the next thing I remember was my name being called so softly, my face being touched softly, my hair being smoothed down and soft humming. I opened my tear-swollen eyes and there they were my three ladies. I sat up and noticed it was getting dark outside. The door to my room was closed. I got up slowly and turned the light on. Then, the four of us sat at my play table and had a tea party. I didn't have any toys, but I had everything I needed whenever my three ladies showed up.

Then, without any warning, my bedroom door opened and slammed against the wall. For some reason, I just calmly turned to my mother, who stood there and I said, "They don't want you in here". When she tried marching over to me in her rage, all three of my ladies stood up and blocked her path. I can't explain it, but my mother could not physically get to me.

Again, calmly I looked at her and said, "They don't

want you in here." I was still doing things for our tea party like I couldn't be bothered with her. She stood there, I think in complete disbelief. She turned around and left, slamming my door behind her.

Sometime shortly after that, I started wetting the bed. I was in so much fear of my mother that I didn't tell her. I found towels and put them over the wet spots. She eventually found out. I imagine due to the smell. She was so furious that she made me sit on the toilet all day long! I wasn't allowed to get up, so I had to be very quiet to stand for a bit. I was on that toilet until well into the night. My brother and father had not been home for a few days.

My mother was 5'3 and close to two hundred pounds by then. I guess that weight happened after her pregnancy failed since she used to be thin. I knew she was coming up the stairs; I could hear her heavy steps. She often came upstairs to slap me and to tell me how stupid I was.

One night when I was in the bathroom, I heard footsteps in the hallway outside the bathroom door. They walked up and down the hallway, back and forth. For some reason, I wasn't scared. When I was done, I washed my hands and then opened the door to return to my bedroom. The hallway was an L shape. The bottom half of the L was between my room and the bathroom. The long part of the L from the bathroom down to their rooms.

As I stepped out, I saw him, a friendly spirit. I wasn't scared, which as an adult, I think it's fascinating how a child innately knows not to be afraid of a friendly spirit. He walked over to me, held out his hand and walked me back to my bed. There he watched as I climbed back into my bed, and went back out to the hallway where he walked up and down. I would hear him most nights and for a while there was peace in my bedroom. Something I wasn't used to. I didn't care that my mother kept me in my room hours upon hours without food or water. When I got thirsty, I snuck to the bathroom and drank out of the faucet.

That peace ended when my father arrived home late one night and barged into my room. I was asleep on my stomach with my arm hanging off the bed when he took me by my wrist and turned me over, demanding I open my mouth. He stuck his penis in my mouth, and this time, I bit down hard, causing him to scream and smack me upside my head until I let go. Holding his crotch, he stumbled back to my doorway.

Something made me jump out of bed, and when he was at the top of the stairs with one foot ready to step down, I pushed him as hard as I could and watched him tumble down the stairs. I don't know what gave me the courage. I went into the bathroom, brushed my teeth, and rinsed my mouth with yellow Listerine. I returned to my room, climbed into bed, and went back to sleep. I would be in my 40s before I felt safe enough to let my arm hang over the side of the bed.

Monsters do exist

After that incident, my father would take me to weird places in church basements where people would put their hands on the top of my head and talk weirdly. They were speaking in tongues. He manipulated people by telling them I was either evil or a chosen one. During my lifetime, this poor excuse for a man would ACT holier than thou on one hand and was nothing more than a _truly evil piece of shit_ in reality. He would go to confession every week, usually dragging me with him to wait in one of the nearby pews.

Nice Lady- the first murder

One night, he brought me to a woman's house who I did not know, left me there, until very late. She was very nice to me. She let me eat all I wanted to. I wasn't used to eating at a kitchen table, especially with an adult! In fact, I was basically controlled with food. That is to say that I rarely got any food. I used to sneak down into our kitchen and steal food while everyone was sleeping. I think I told that nice lady about that because I remember telling her about the squeaks on the floor that I avoided by stepping around them.

He brought me to her house a few more times after that. She asked me if it was true that I pushed my daddy down the stairs. I told her I was never allowed to call him daddy. Yes, I did push him down the stairs. She asked me why since I was such a nice, well-behaved child. I told her because he stuck his thing in my mouth, and he had done that so many other times before, but that was the last time he did it because I bit him. While she hugged me, she spoke out loud, asking God's heavenly angels to protect me. That night when he came to pick me up, they had an argument on her front porch while I waited in his car.

I'm not sure how long after that it was until he took me to visit her in the hospital. She was so happy to see me and gave me a little hug the best she could as she was in her bed, halfway sitting up. He walked to the other side of her bed. I remember her face changing as if she didn't like seeing him. She said a lot of stuff to him he clearly didn't like. I heard a lot of God and Jesus and angels and Satan from her soft-spoken voice. (I would learn throughout the years that he loved manipulating women, but God help the woman that calls him out on his lies and bullshit.)

I watched his face change in front of me, from his fake smile to his scary, dark look. I looked back and forth from him to her. When she could see I was trembling in fear, she gently took my hand and told me everything was ok. She began telling him that she believed everything I told her. She told him she wasn't scared of his threats of being sued. He interrupted her and demanded I leave the room and wait out in the hallway pointing to the door, with his dark look and scary voice.

I went out into the hallway. I got scared, so I opened the door a crack, and what I witnessed I never told a soul for over forty years. He had a pillow over her face, and her arms were outstretched as she was still in the sitting up position in the hospital bed. His back was to me as he pushed down on the pillow, and her arms were reaching for him. Her feet were kicking at the end of the bed under the sheet.

I don't know how long it went on. It seemed like forever. But then she stopped moving. I closed the door a little bit and sat down quietly in the chair, rocking back and forth even though it wasn't a rocking chair. The door suddenly opened wide, and my father was calling very calmly for someone. Then the nurses came down the hall. I don't remember any beeps or noises. It was all so silent. With the door open and all of the commotion going on, I stood up and watched my father. He put on his religious act for the staff, saying how one minute they were talking about life, and the next thing he knew, she was reaching her arms out and called out Jesus' name, then died. I was too scared to look at her, but when my father saw me looking at him from the doorway, he stopped talking. He used me at that moment to excuse himself. We left the hospital. I had wet my pants.

When we got back to the Troy St house, he decided the family needed to go camping. But we didn't take the motorhome or my brother; it was just me. My brother stayed with friends. They packed up the station wagon and hooked up the brand-new Reinell motorboat. It was early morning when we drove up to the San Juan Islands. They would talk very quietly but angrily to each other in the front seat of the red station wagon. Then, there would be silence for a long time. They made me sit in the very back.

I was scared. The drive felt like forever.

When we got on the boat, we drove on the water for a long time. We never saw a soul, and I remember being really, really scared. It was very quiet. Too quiet. I eventually fell asleep under the bow of the boat, in a cubby. Then, my parents began arguing once again. Most arguments I heard had my name in it.

My father told me I was going for a swim. My parents were arguing even more, and I became even more afraid. My father turned suddenly. In one move, he grabbed me and threw me into the water where I began treading water. There wasn't anyone else around, and it was too far to swim to an island that I saw in the distance. I didn't have a life jacket on. I was out there treading water for some time as they sat on the boat some distance away.

From what I could tell, they were not even looking in my direction. It was so quiet except for their occasional outbreak of arguing. Then out of nowhere, there was a boat with a man and a woman on it. I heard their engine shut off, and they glided up to me. The woman was at the open bow of their boat and asked me my name in a very sweet and calming voice. I told her my name while I continued treading water and shivering from being cold. I was extremely tired. She told me to stay right there, that they would bring the boat closer to me, and to just keep doing what I was doing.

Then the woman went back and took the wheel of their boat while the man came to the side of the boat. He said my name softly, told me he was taking me out of the water, and with a gentle swoop, he did. Both of them frantically checked my body over, turning me around and around, talking to each other with calm voices. Then they put a big towel around me. Thats when my parents' boat came over, and when the man realized they were my parents, he began yelling at them.

My mother did not say a word, and my father had his fake laugh. He was laughing at this man. Right before the man picked up his CB radio, he said to my father, " It's a miracle she wasn't killed!" My father had thrown me into a swarm of jellyfish! I "wasn't stung even once by some miracle," the man said angrily.

The man was making a call on his CB radio when my mother drove up close alongside their boat. My father jumped onto their boat and grabbed me. I don't remember what happened after that. I know they didn't bring me back to the Troy St. house.

1976

Later, when I was nine years old, I asked them why they did that to me? Again, I won't forget the look between them. I was told they "don't remember that EVER happening" and for me to "stop making up lies."

Around that time, I would find a picture on my father's nightstand of me sitting in a highchair with my feet bandaged, with a weird look on my face. My mother had told me to go find something she needed out of that drawer. I brought her the picture instead and asked her why I looked so weird? It took a lot of courage to ask, but at nine years old, I already knew my mother hated me, I knew I would get beaten, but something made me ask anyway.

It was the look on her face that would stay with me forever. Little did I know that it was a puzzle piece I'd need to help me heal in the future. The reality of my memory scared them! She asked me where I got the picture from. Then told me I was a fucking idiot because I was supposed to go to HER nightstand. I told her I recognized the kitchen from our lake house cabin in Virginia.

"You remember the cabin?" she asked in a very pissed-off tone.

"Yes, I do," I told her. She snatched the picture out of my hand and slapped me hard across my face, then she sent me to my room, where I would stay for the rest of the day and go another night without any dinner.

A Safe Shelter- A friend – Some Good Memories

One day when I was 6 or 7 and my mother was out, my father came to my bedroom with a little suitcase, and packed up some of my things. I asked him where we were going, but he didn't answer me. We got into his car. We drove around awhile until eventually I fell asleep. I woke up to his mean voice telling me, to get up. We were parked in front of a set of stairs that led up to a big stone building. Someone came to the door to let us in. It must have been very late because no one was around until the sweetest face I had ever seen with a bright smile came down the hallway. She was a Nun dressed in her black and white attire.

The next thing I remember is this nun asking if she could hold my hand while she took me upstairs. I don't think I even questioned why I was there or even cared about my father. In fact, I didn't even care to say goodbye. I wasn't afraid for some reason. She turned on the lights, and they were very bright. My eyes took everything in. It was a large room with several curtains that wrapped around each little bed to give some privacy. The nun guided me to the other side of the room where she showed me my bed and introduced herself as Sister Teresa, our room mother.

I pointed to the big brown wooden box that reached from the floor to the ceiling and had a door, next to what would be my bed. She explained to me that it was her bedroom. I would sleep on this side of her bedroom and on the other side was a little girl my age from Germany. She told me her name was Tammy. But, I needed to go to sleep because it was late, and we didn't want to wake up all the other little girls. She helped me put my PJs on, and when she saw my bruised body, I heard her sigh, and then she told me I'd be safe here.

I was at Saint Mary's Catholic Boarding School for girls. Grades one through twelve. Sister Agnes was our principle. This would be the only time in my childhood that I would actually feel safe every single day. I may have been in first or second grade. I'm not sure. That first morning, I was awakened by a bell and our nun swinging open all of the curtains that went around each bed, with a big smile. I was introduced to Tammy, who was told to show me around and show me what to do. Immediately, Tammy and I became inseparable friends. I was never allowed to have friends. Tammy was my first friend, ever!

That morning, I followed her out to the hallway, where each girl was on their knees saying the quick morning prayer. Afterwards, we went into our large bathroom, where there were individual little sinks for kids. We washed our faces, brushed our teeth, and then returned to our room where my new uniform was laid nicely out on my bed. I got dressed quickly, and then waited for Tammy.

We went downstairs to the cafeteria for breakfast. Thats where Sister Teresa told me I could eat as much as I wanted. I was a little child that didn't weigh much. My mother frequently called me a scrawny, stupid, and klutzy kid. We then went to the classroom, where I met my new teacher. School had already been in session but I'm not sure how many months in. I remember my teacher being very nice to me, because I was a little behind in the studies. But I was able to make that up quickly and that seemed to make my teacher very happy.

After school was the best part! St Mary's sat on a large

piece of land. Behind the school was a huge indoor swimming pool, and outside the pool was a rack filled with bicycles! On my first day, I was given a bathing suit. I put it on and then ran and jumped into the deep end of the pool and started treading water. Tammy jumped in next to me, and then we heard a whistle. Thankfully, we didn't get in trouble. I was just told the rules. Tammy and I were the only first graders who got to swim in the deep end, and we loved it! After school, we could go get a snack and then play for a few hours. We either rode bikes or went swimming. It was a beautiful, carefree, and safe place. I was happy and felt safe for the first time in my young life! We rarely saw the older girls, and when we went to church, that's the only place we saw the priest. There were no men on our campus that I had ever seen, and I liked that a lot.

One Sunday, Sister Teresa told me I had to put on a new dress my father sent over because he was picking me up for the afternoon. I didn't know, hadn't cared how long it had been since I saw him last, but I did not want to go. I cried and told her I didn't want to put on that awful dress, with the short lacy white socks and black patterned shoes.

Sister Teresa asked me why. I got very quiet, and then in a soft, barely audible voice, I told her I didn't like what happened to me when I wore those kinds of dresses.

She didn't make me put on the dress. Instead, she found some pants, a shirt, and a pair of *Keds* and then walked me to the same foyer where I came in that first night. She sat with me on the long wooden bench, holding my tiny hand until he arrived. He was always late. He was late or didn't show up for everything in my childhood.

He was clearly angry that I wasn't in the dress when he finally got there. This must have been outside visiting hours since she reminded him of that. Across the road was a Kmart. We drove over there where my father met with a man. They argued, and my father drove me back to the school. I had peed in my pants. I got out of the car and ran up the stairs without even looking back. Sister Teresa was standing there to greet me. She held her arms open, and I hugged her. I knew I was safe being back at St. Mary's.

I'm not sure how long I was there, but I know I was happy. I never asked about my parents, and I certainly never missed them. No, I didn't even think about them. Looking back, I believe somehow Sister Teresa got me out of a lot of visits. For years, I had a story that I told of spending several years at that school when, in fact, I didn't. It was just one year and it was the happiest place in my entire childhood. I think because I was so happy there and had so many blanks in my memory that it was a coping mechanism for me.

Then one Sunday, I was told I absolutely had to visit with my parents and brother. Sister Teresa was shocked I had a brother and asked a few questions. I told her he was my parents' favorite, and when I was at home, I was kept separate from him. She gave me a big, loving hug.

They all three pulled up in a new station wagon. In the car was our black Lab Pokey and a new German Shepard puppy being held by my mother in the front seat. My brother was in the back seat looking out the window at the big building. My heart sank. I didn't want to go. I hugged Sister Teresa and walked slowly down the stairs. My father yelled for me to hurry up. I wouldn't know it at the time, but when I climbed into the backseat, it would be the last time I would see Tammy, Sister Teresa, or the school. My parents never even picked my things up from the school. We drove to the farmhouse where my mother left me with my father as she took the dogs, my brother and left. He made me drink something and swallow a pill. It was happening again. I was no longer safe.

☐

Woodburn - No longer safe

I woke up to men's voices downstairs. They were loud, laughing, and then I heard mumbling. I had been sleeping on a bunkbed, the bottom bunk. I could hear footsteps coming up so I closed my eyes and scrunched my body up. The door opened, and I heard a scuffling above me. I didn't even know someone was up there. I heard a girl's voice and two men laughing. I was too scared to open my eyes. She was crying out when they dragged her away. I don't know how long she was down there. But I could hear her crying. I could hear her begging them to stop. I could hear a man's voice saying they didn't like that.

It seemed like forever when they returned her to the room and turned on the light. I heard her climb into the top bunk. When they left, I slowly rolled over onto my back, looking at the bottom of the blue and gray striped mattress above. The moon was shining through the window, and I could see a wet spot forming above me.

She was gone in the morning when I woke up. I never even knew what she looked like. (I often wonder if she survived that night in that house in Woodburn, Oregon.)

After selling the Portland house, the family resided in Woodburn. It was a two-story farmhouse with two chimneys at the top. The carpet was weird because it was all different colors. It was as if all the pieces were samples from a carpet store. The dining room, living room, and kitchen were downstairs, with a guest bedroom and bathroom.

Upstairs were three bedrooms and a bathroom. There was a long driveway that led up to the house, and it sat on three acres. I don't remember the street name, but exactly one mile up the straight, flat road sat a little white Catholic Church. My mother hated that house because she was often scared. For some reason my mother let me out of my room to be downstairs where she was. I remember being in the kitchen when she turned around with something in her hand and dropped it. I was sitting at the table eating a bowl of cereal. I don't know how to explain that when I saw ghosts or spirits as a child, I didn't know they were ghosts. I was never scared. It was kind of normal for me.

That particular day, there was a man and woman sitting with me. They were kind. Or I should say they felt kind. They didn't speak; they just watched me. That's what my mother saw when she dropped whatever she was holding. My mother asked me if I saw anything unusual. I looked at her and then at them. Then I simply said to her that, "They live here. This is their house." She didn't like that answer, and when she came towards me to hit me, there was a big crash behind her. The stack of plates had come off the shelf and broke on the floor. I saw the woman standing there by the plates, and the man was by me. My mother screamed at me to go to my room.

When my father came home, they had another argument. My entire childhood was them arguing and fighting with my name always in their conversation. I could not understand why they adopted me and hated me so much! That night, my father dragged me to another of his weird prayer meetings where I was told by strangers that I was evil and they had to "pray" the evil away. It was so confusing to me, and the people freaked me out!

Much of my childhood was filled with me being told that I was a bad child. I was only called by my name in public. Otherwise, I was addressed as, "hey dummy" by my father and "fucking little cunt" and "little bastard" by my mother. But let's throw in some church bullshit now with my parents making ME go to confession. The only time in my childhood that I had respect for the catholic church and felt safe in a church was at Saint Mary's school for girls.

One day, when I was 8 or 9, we were at the farmhouse. I don't know why we called it a farmhouse because it wasn't a working farm (we had two Black Angus steers). My mother and brother were gone when a big truck pulled up and drove into the field. My father insisted I go out with him to the truck. I had no idea what was going on, but I put on my little green rubber boots and walked out. The man took out a rifle and shot one of the black Angus cows. I watched it fall. Then he drove the truck over to where the side of it opened, and he took a big cable with a large hook on it. This is where I draw a blank because the next thing I remember was my father with his big black and silver Buck knife, cutting up the steer that hung there. I looked down at my little green rubber boots that were in a pool of blood, and I fainted. I had seen my father cut something large up when I was at the lake house when I was younger. I only remember voices and blood. I would mention those two situations when I was around 11 years old and told it was just my imagination and to stop making up stories.

While residing at that house in Woodburn, my father wrote a " Childrens" book entitled Pierre Le Possum. It never got published. It was about a possum and a fox who got an invitation to see the king. It was also about how much abuse the possum endured along the trip, but the fox had an easy path. At the end of the book, the possum gets killed by going over a waterfall and drowning and "Goes to the kingdom of God." I wouldn't realize it at the time because I was so young, but I knew enough that I was meant to be the stupid possum and my brother was the fox. It was right there in writing.

When I was in my thirties, my father mailed it to me. This arrogant, manipulative, piece of shit, poor excuse for a man, wrote about me being killed, but my brain wouldn't let me see it clearly until years later. I was angry that he wrote about the fantasy of killing me. I was angry because he knew my mother gave me horrible beatings that he did nothing about. I was angry about a lot of things that happened.

When we were in Woodburn, there was a man who brought us a Shetland pony. I was outside with the dogs.

My brother and parents would claim the German Shepard was my brother's. His name was Tomah, and he followed me everywhere. Tomah also saw the ghost couple in the house, and I remember the feeling that they liked him. Anyway, this man unloaded the pony from the trailer, and my father turned to me with his fake laugh to tell me it was mine. I remember the surprised look on the man's face, and then the man said something like it was a work pony, not a child's pony. I still remember the man's face of concern.

My brother got a horse that was beautiful and gentle that he barely rode. I got a pony that I was forced to ride. It would run so fast that I couldn't control him, and then he would put his head down and buck me off. He threw me into barbed wire fences. He threw me against the barn. He threw me into trees; he threw me so much the neighbors were concerned and expressed that to my parents. Anytime anyone would express concern for me throughout my childhood, they were threatened with being sued.

My other Grandmother Paula was my adoptive mother's mother, whom I loved. She was nothing like my mother. She was sweet to me, and her house was so welcoming.

She was married to Tommy, her second husband after she had been widowed. Tommy was the only Grandfather I knew. He was a very happy man that swung me around and played with me. He was killed in a car accident.

My mother hated the fact that Grandmother Paula and I got along so well. Years later, I would learn that every letter she sent to me was thrown away. The same way birthday and holiday gifts were. I was told that my Grandmother no longer loved me because I was a terrible child. But fortunately, I found my Grandmother when I was in my thirties, and she was so happy to hear from me! We cleared everything up. Grandmother Paula died not long after that. I had no idea she was sick.

Then, one day, the dreaded grandmother came out for a visit. This is the Grandmother who hated me. Her name was Lenore, and of course, I was afraid of her, and I stayed away, hiding wherever I could. My mother and brother avoided her and went to the lake house, leaving me with my father and Lenore.

One morning, my father ordered me to ride my bike down the driveway as fast as I could. He and Lenore were sitting on the front porch having coffee. I think I was maybe close to nine years old, and by this time, Tomah followed me everywhere. I didn't want to ride my bike. I knew something was up because of his stupid fake laugh. He got very angry and again ordered me to go. So off I went, but he held on to Tomah. I figured I would just take off and ride down to the church, something I did often to escape.

Off I went, and when I was almost at the end of the driveway, he yelled my name so loud and sharp, it scared me, and I turned around. That's when it happened, instant pain followed by fear! Tomah witnessed it and came charging down the driveway to be with me. I was hanging on barbwire by my neck and screaming in pain. My father had strung a piece of barbed wire across the driveway, horizontally, without any red or orange safety flags on it. He had never done that before, so I didn't expect it. When he called my name, and I turned my head to the right, the wire was exactly at my neck's height, while sitting on the banana seat of my purple Schwinn bicycle. The barbed wire went into the left side of my neck, and my bike flew out and up. Like I was popping a wheelie. There I hung, screaming in pain, while only my knees were on the ground in a weird way. The wire was so tight in my neck, I was too scared and confused to move.

Someone was driving by and got out to help. I was hanging there on barbed wire! The man unhooked the wire from the fence and gently got the barbed part out of my neck. Then he checked me over to make sure I was okay. All this was done before my father got to me. My father was taking his time to get to me. It is interesting that Tomah allowed a strange man to help me, but wouldn't let my father near me. He growled at him and would not let him touch me.

What I remember was his stupid laugh and how "accident prone" he told the man I was. "Accident prone?" the man said, "This was not an accident; this was carelessness." Then my father told the man an outright lie and told him he told me not to ride my bike down the driveway. How I knew it was the day of the week when the horses ate the grass along the driveway.

It was a pure lie. We had three acres and the horses NEVER ate along the driveway, NEVER! In fact, they never ate there AFTER my accident either. Also, he must have been up pretty early to put that wire there without me noticing what he was doing. (I was never taken to the hospital, and I still have a scar on my neck and up along my face. The face scar looks like a deep wrinkle, and I'm okay with that.) When I made it back up to the house, I looked at my grandmother sitting in the chair with her cane. Through my tears, I told her how my father lied to that man. She told me my father warned her I lied all the time.

At that young age, I suddenly felt a rage bubble up in me, and at that moment, I decided I hated Lenore. I hated these two people claiming to be my parents! I hated my brother that, whenever he was around me, would punch me and hurt me every time! I hated this "family" that I somehow got unlucky enough to be adopted in! I hated this grandmother! I don't know if I ever felt hate like that for all of them before that moment.

What my father did next was unbearable. He loaded me and Tomah in the car. We drove to a veterinary office, and I was forced to watch my dog be put to sleep! My father claimed he was dangerous! We never even brought Tomah home to be buried. (For years, he would claim Tomah almost bit a neighbor girl and was forced to have him put down. I was too afraid to tell the truth because my mother loved Tomah.)

☐

A Little Power and Happiness

I believe this is when I began my sneaky passive aggressiveness. For the next few days, while Lenore was visiting, I did things like put just enough lotion on the bathroom door handle so she couldn't open it easily. I put just enough salt in her tea to question, but not know. I hid her cane every chance I got, but where she "found" it where she first looked. I turned on the hot water full blast when she was taking a shower and then pretended I had been outside in the barn.

Nothing could ever be proven when she complained to my father about it, and my mother and brother were still not home. When he would have his back to me, I would give her a little smirk, and she would point her stupid cane at me. When my father would turn around, I would put my head down and say, "She hates me because I'm adopted." It was the truth; she hated me. Yes, torturing this woman like this for a few days brought me lots of happiness and a sense of power.

I have never forgotten that day at the lake in Virginia

when I was three. It would take time before I could truly get under her skin. You see, it's this adopted one who would see Lenore's true character and the truth about her dead husband. Something that she made happen for her own reasons. A simple fucking background check, Virginia! There were so many red flags with these two "parents" - it should have been a flashing warning red banner!

You failed to do your job, Virginia

By 1976, the money exchange with the strange men stopped. But drugging me did not. Every time we went anywhere as a family, I was forced to swallow pills and drink Vicks 44 cough syrup. Sometimes, the pills would be put in chunks of cantaloupe or Honey dew melon. (To this day, I hate the smell of those.) I would wake up in the motor home all alone. Or in a tent by myself.

I remember one time when this nice family was camping next to us at a lake, and they must have witnessed me being all alone. They had kids older than me but they were nice too. It was a happy family. I was too embarrassed when they offered me food but I was so hungry, and they insisted I eat. I hung out and played with them all day. It was the first time I saw what a "normal" family was like. I watched how they interacted with each other. How pleasant they were to each other and, I noticed how there was no yelling, screaming or cursing. I watched how the mom and dad hugged their kids.

They asked me about my scar, and I hung my head in embarrassment while I told them with as little detail as possible. I still remember their reaction, shock, and then compassion. The kids asked me if I wanted to go swimming with them so I went to our tent to put my swim suit on. I still remember the shock on their faces as my bruises were showing now. My family would be gone that entire day. Boating around the lake, eating at the marina, gone all day. When it got dark, I was sitting around the campfire roasting hotdogs with this wonderful family. They showed me how to do it, and it was fun. Then, they showed me how to roast marshmallows to make s'mores. I loved it, being with such nice people!

I must have fallen asleep because when I woke up, I heard raised voices. I had a warm blanket around me. My parents were arguing with this nice and clearly concerned couple. The words "accident prone" and "problem child" came out of my mother's mouth, but the couple defended me. I didn't realize it at the time, but this family could see I was obviously physically and emotionally abused. I remember the woman defending me by saying what a well-behaved, enjoyable child I was, and then she said something that would stay with me forever.

"It is your responsibility to take care of this beautiful child." Then she said, " What if there was a pervert here and not us? You left your child all alone to defend herself." That's when the words of being sued and the normal routine of threats came out. My father yanked me out of the chair, dragging me away. I said thank you to the family and, "I'm adopted." My parents packed up and we left shortly after. I remember the word "beautiful" being used to describe me, and I smiled. I wasn't used to being described like that before. I was used to being called "fucking little cunt" and "fucking little bastard" and "dummy." I was used to being called "ugly and stupid". I was used to being told I was "worthless" and I "wouldn't amount to anything." I was never told anything positive about myself.

We were living at the farmhouse in Woodburn when at some point I realized that my father was rarely home and when he was, the yelling and screaming never ended. There was absolutely no love between my parents. I couldn't even tell you when their anniversary was. I couldn't tell you who was at their wedding. There were no pictures of their wedding, and the few times I asked my mother to see them, I got beat or slapped.

That was the norm when I asked questions. Questions about the strange men. Questions about things that happened to me while living at the Portland house. I was beaten by her and he would say I was crazy and too young to have any real memories. She never beat me in front of him but she would save it for the moment he left the house.

By 1976, I was nine years old, had been to so many different schools, and I think that I haven't finish a grade. Then came Sacred Heart in Woodburn, where I was miserable. I couldn't understand why the nuns were so mean! But there was some sense of routine in my young life, and even though I was scared there, I knew I was going to be okay.

Now, the strange thing about my father always being gone. No, he wasn't working. He wasn't a hard working attorney. In fact, I would find out years later that he didn't pass the Bar Exam and get his Oregon Attorney's license until 1976 when I was nine. That would be another simmering moment in my life, him not working and always being gone. Not that it was a bad thing for him to be away from me, but that meant I was left with my mother who beat me.

I started and finished fourth grade and began fifth grade when my parents announced that we were moving. It was the late 70's. My mother said it was because of the weather, which was constantly overcast. For some reason, I didn't believe her, even though there were a lot of overcast days.

☐

Bend, Oregon- Sixth Grade

Our new location was Bend, Oregon. When we arrived in the car, I recognized Mt. Bachelor and asked my parents if we had ever been there before. The look between them was the normal look whenever I asked questions they didn't like. I didn't get an answer, so I just looked out the window. When we pulled up to *The River House Hotel,* I was so excited. Coming from Woodburn, there weren't any lakes or rivers, and this hotel was on the beautiful Deschutes River. Our room had a little kitchen in it, but the best part was the indoor heated swimming pool. I was in heaven! Bend was absolutely beautiful and the sky had a brilliant color of blue!

I was completely thrilled that I no longer had to go to Catholic school! Apparently, it only went up to fifth grade, and my mother said it was best to mingle with the public school kids now. My mother signed me up for class at *Kenwood Elementary.* I remember mother saying how my previous school must have lost my paperwork. They put me in the classroom across from the office. When I entered fifth grade I had loved math in school, but here I was behind, way behind. It was November. I would struggle with math after that. I was always too scared to ask any teacher for help, even though I had some nice teachers. It would be a pattern for a long time, never asking for help. My parents had never, and I mean NEVER, helped me with any of my homework or school projects. It's humorous to me now; one time we had to make papier mâché animals. I would say mine was an adorable panda. In reality, it was a bit of a blob with four nubs, painted black and white. I think I got a B for effort, most likely from the kindness of my teacher.

Bend, Oregon at that time including its entire border was only about 10,000 people. So, it was considered a small town. There was a downtown area with a *JC Penny's* along with other shops and the *Tower movie theater*. I liked it right away. I didn't care that my brother was driven to and from his school, and I had to walk about a mile to and from my school. I liked having sidewalks. I got to look at everything along the way.

We lived at that hotel for over a month because our house in The West Hills wasn't empty yet. I remember the first time I saw that house. It was beautiful. It sat on the corner up on a hill. It had a huge fenced backyard with a big pine tree in the middle. There were thirteen steps up to the front porch that overlooked the street and the old logging road that led straight down to *Kenwood Elementary*. The house was built in the 1940s and was immaculate. There was even carpet in the kitchen, which I had never seen carpet in a kitchen before. It was originally a two-bedroom house. My parents' room had a bathroom, and then there was a bathroom in the hall that also connected to my brothers' room. On the other side of the house was an added washroom and a tiny room with a closet. That was my room. Completely away from the rest of the family by the back door. There was also a door between the kitchen and my room that was closed off. My room didn't have any heat.

When we moved in and got settled, I started to notice all these family photos with only my brother in them. There were no pictures of me. I had found a box of Polaroid pictures, and one day, I was looking in there for pictures of me and could only find one. I was reading something at school. All these polaroids were in a box of vacations on the water, camping, skiing, and so on. Nothing with me.

When I got to the bottom of the box, I saw a picture that someone had taken at Lenore's house and sent to my parents. I was guessing that I must have been about seven years old, and it must have been when we visited both grandmothers. I was in a red, white, and blue striped bathing suit and smiling. I don't know who took the picture, but I looked happy. I was adorable!

Later, my memory took me back to how people would sometimes comment on what a beautiful child I was. I asked my mother one day why there were no pictures of me. She grabbed my neck with her fingernails so fast that I couldn't run. With complete hate and rage, she looked me in the eye and told me it was because I was "fucking ugly." I was used to her cursing, name-calling, being beaten, punched, and ridiculed.

I did enjoy living in that neighborhood. There were lots of kids my age running around in an undeveloped area with lots of trees behind our house and up the street.

It's important to include the fact that my father, with his law degree and being from the east coast, got the job as an Assistant District Attorney. It was a "new start" for my parents they explained, not to me, but to my brother. New start? I knew they despised each other. I also knew instinctively, it would not last. But Bend welcomed us and I even had my picture in the paper playing around at school. My mother beat me badly for that picture; she told me that my brother deserved to be in the paper, not me! But, I didn't care. It was worth it.

That same school year, I began asking questions about things I remembered from when I was younger and unfortunately, I made the mistake of asking about the lady in the hospital who took care of me. I really pushed it because I was a kid wanting answers. I made the mistake of saying, "You know, the one that reached for Jesus?" We were in the living room. My brother was at a friend's house, and it was just the three of us. My mother looked at me in silence and then a dark glare at my father. I was sent to my room. Later that night, my father would come into my room and ask me what I remembered. I just said I remember how nice she was to me. But I could see that he knew that I knew something, and immediately I was frightened. He left my room and slammed my door shut.

Unwelcome Stranger

A few nights later, a noise woke me up. As usual, my twin bed was against the wall under the one window. It sounded like someone was trying to open the window! I got as close to the wall as I could get, feeling how cold it was. I was so scared I couldn't move. Then I heard a calming unfamiliar voice that said my name and then said, RUN! I popped out of bed screaming, and when I got out my door, the next door between my room and the kitchen was blocked. I completely freaked out until both parents came to see what was happening.

I told them somebody tried breaking into my room. My mother got mad and yelled at me to stop lying. Then my father did his fake laugh and told me to settle down. My mother looked at my father and then walked into my room. She turned on the lights and looked out the window. The screen had been cut and my window was open about two inches. The look on my mother's face was real surprise. I asked why the police were not called?

My father did his stupid fake laugh and said I must have opened the window and the screen was already like that. I looked out that window every day, and it was clear that the cut was brand new. I wouldn't have opened the window since it was too cold at night and my room did not have heat. I moved to the other side of the house to sleep in the living room the rest of the night.

The next day, I got ready for school. I would walk with my neighbor, who was the same age. Her mom and stepdad were really nice people and owned a store downtown. My mother had actually made a friend, and for a short time, she didn't beat me as much after school. I stayed out of her way, but I knew it wouldn't last. I had never known my mother to have any friends.

That day, my neighbor and I were walking home from school straight up the old dirt logging road that ended at our street. We noticed an old, dirty white station wagon following us. We both thought it was weird because the road had potholes, and no cars were used since there was another paved road. I got home and forgot all about it. The next day, I got the idea to ride my bicycle. My friend got on the back, and off we went. It was downhill most of the way to school. Then, we would take turns pushing it up the hill back home after school. This went on for a few days, and each day, we would see this car with a creepy-looking guy in it. One day we actually ran the last bit to her house and told her mom. In retrospect, my mother probably told my friends that I was a liar who made up stories for attention because I could see her mom didn't believe us. I say this because in my heart I know this woman wouldn't have left me to walk home on my own the next day after school.

I didn't ride my bike that day, and my friend's mom picked her up early for a dentist appointment. I was alone walking up the hill, when out of nowhere that same car appeared with that same creepy man! He opened his door to grab me. I might have been little, but I was strong. I fought him, and I bit him hard on his arm. I was screaming when someone came out of their house. I ran all the way home, screaming and crying. I was in shock. My mother didn't care and called me a "fucking liar."

I would find out years later that, there were people who noticed that car and had called the police a few times. On that day, several people were looking for me. The police were called and he was arrested with equipment to dispose of a body. Tape, plastic bags, and a hacksaw. He claimed he was hired by the assistant district attorney to get rid of his troubled adopted daughter. No one believed him because the assistant district attorney (ADA) had recently put this guy's brother behind bars for twenty years. That ADA was my asshole father. I never walked that road alone again. I was not allowed to talk to the police. I was not allowed to talk about it at home or at school. I never did. I was too scared.

Junior High

I was in Junior High School when my father bought a house next to the health food store and across from a grocery store. He bought it and converted it into a Law Office. I asked him why, since he worked at the courthouse. His fake laugh came out, and then he got mad and told me to mind my own business. It was then I started to notice looks from people around town and feel a certain energy. If we went out to dinner, there were always looks and hushed voices if we walked by. No one greeted us like before. I learned later that he got fired from his DA position for nefarious reasons.. I was forced to go to church on Sundays with my father. My brother and mother did not go. Before moving to Bend, I don't remember going to church every Sunday.

We were always late, and in his arrogance, he would march us right up front while the service was in full swing, right in front of the Priest. My father was so arrogant, and I was always so embarrassed. Everything he did was for his own purpose. He wanted to be seen. Something I wouldn't understand until years later. People changed towards me after he "left" the courthouse. It was an energy I felt from people until I grew up and left Bend.

It was Springtime, and one day out of the blue, my father showed up. He was never home and basically showed up when he wanted to. That particular day, he would insist on me going with him to give my mother a break. A break from what? Beating me? I thought to myself. Back then to a kid, Redmond seemed far away, but it was only twenty miles. He would park the car and make me wait inside it. Sometimes for hours and, I mean hours. I was used to it. Sometimes I just feel asleep. Sometimes I got bored and followed him without him seeing me. One time, I got angry waiting, went into Rexall Drug store and bought a milkshake.

Another Murder

There was a murder that took place in Bend, Oregon, in April, 1979. Shortly before the article came out, my brother was in the front seat of my father's cream-colored two-door Oldsmobile. I was in the back seat. My brother needed to put the seat back. He pulled out a short reddish wig. Out came the fake laugh, but I knew who wore that wig. I didn't know her name, but I saw her through a window. Instinctively, I knew something was wrong and got scared. The mere fact that I was with both of them at the same time. Something was up; I felt it.

That day, he drove my brother and I down to Drake Park while he did his act of being a religious man. It was an act I had been around my entire childhood. There were people there, and I just walked over to the flock of Canadian Geese. They always went after my father, but not me. I knew I was safe around those geese. This day would stick with me. The woman who was murdered looked like his secretary. She was missing.

I was thirty-eight years old when I went back to Bend, spoke to a former neighbor, and found out the truth. My father had been harassing his secretary at the courthouse. She was engaged to a sheriff at the time and had absolutely no feelings for my father. He upped the ante by breaking into her place and was caught jerking off in her closet when she went home for lunch. Why in the HELL was he NOT arrested? He was fired but suffered no other consequences. Nothing was done to him! He was just able to leave and live his life.

My father taunted the DA and the police after he was fired. He knew he would never get caught, and he never did. He knew if I ever said anything, I would just look like a liar and crazy. I told the police all those years later that I was positive he made contact with those undercover cops. I knew he did it. He did other horrible things and kept those women's jewelry. On the anniversary of the day the police thought she had been killed, Bill and his friend, the ONLY friend I knew him to have, were in the park bible-thumping to anyone who walked by.

He loved to flaunt what he got away with, and I suspect that his friend knew and maybe saw something. He may have been catholic but his cover was that he was deeply religious. It was all bull shit. That friend of his? I heard a few years later that he wound up in a mental institution. I went to school with one of his children. And yes, years later I did tell the police what I knew but nothing was done. I'm sure they were told the same old thing, that I told stories? □

1979 -12 Years Old

I was in my room reading one afternoon, when unexpectedly my father came home. I could smell something gross on his breath and shivered physically when I saw his eyes. I was twelve, going on thirteen and I got so scared. I had no one to protect me, so I had to protect myself. When he went into my parents' room I ran to the living room closet and got the hunting rifle and ammo that was kept there. I knew how to load it because he took my brother and I out to shoot it once, along with a 38 revolver. I took them into my bedroom and shut the door.

I sat down along the wall facing my door with the loaded rifle across my lap. The screaming rose from my parents' room, and then I heard the bedroom door slam. He was heading my way, I knew it. I stood up, and when he opened my door angrily, I was ready for him. He looked at me with those mean drunken eyes and did his fake laugh.

"What are you going to do? Shoot me?" he said in a mocking tone. I had already cocked the rifle. I took one step forward. Aiming it at him, looking him straight into his wicked dark eyes and not saying a word. I WAS ready to kill him. I was 12 years old, and I was ready to kill this piece of shit, poor excuse for a man. Then he took a step backward. This time, his laugh was nervous; he knew I was serious.

He didn't say a word; he just left the house. I would spend an entire year blocking my door and sleeping with that loaded rifle. Every morning, I would go out to the garage and hide it before catching the school bus, and every night, I would go retrieve it before I went to bed.

Early 80's

It was the spring in the early 80s when my mother finally got tired of him never coming home. It was a Saturday morning, and someone called her about her husband. I don't know what was said but my mother threw his suits and all his clothes out onto the front yard. Then she had the locks changed. Some neighbor must have called him because he rushed home. He moved into his office permanently.

Her only friend the neighbor had just moved to Portland.

My mother's anger just got worse. He was an attorney, and she was in a hopeless situation.

Life was complete hell for me at home, more so than ever. Every day, the beatings got worse. I was so brainwashed into not defending myself that I just took it. The worst part? We had PE every day. Each day, they would make us take a shower and then line up naked to get a towel from our PE teacher. I was always covered in bruises, scratches, cuts and NO ONE did a damn thing to help me.

I love sports. Swim practice after school was a great way to stay away from my house. I even walked three or more miles home just so I could delay being there.

Freshman in High School- 15 - 1982

By the time I was a freshman in high school, it was unbearable at home with mother. My father conned me into moving into a house he had rented. I didn't care. I just couldn't take the beatings anymore. Me moving in was for his bull shit act for a woman he had his eye on. He was cruising the Christian churches for the perfect cover. A stupid woman that he could control. He finally found one when I was fifteen years old. He had already filled her head about me because the moment I met her, I immediately felt an energy from her that she covered with a fake smile. She didn't like me, and I didn't like her. She was one of those women who thought she was marrying into money because he was a lawyer, and I was in the way. (In reality, he sucked as a lawyer.) Her kids were all grown. My father took her skiing and all kinds of sporting things to do, leaving me alone for days at a time. Never calling to check on me. But I didn't care; I liked him being gone.

Poison

Then my father insisted I start drinking apple juice at night. I didn't like it. It was too sweet for me. One day, I came home from swim practice when he insisted I drink the apple juice in front of his stupid girlfriend, telling her how healthy it was for me. He knew I wouldn't argue with him in front of her. Within an hour, I was broken out in hives. I didn't know what was in the juice that caused hives, and he had left for the night.

I was miserable as the hives got worse. He came home the next day, and I insisted he take me to the doctor or I would call a friend's mom to take me. He took me to Doctor M., who was an old man who went to our church, and I didn't want him to even touch me. He creeped me out, and he reminded me of someone, I just didn't know who. This doctor was a reminder of a strange man experience. He explained that I must have eaten something that I had an allergic reaction to and sent me home with medicine. The hives went away, but I felt worse, and my father again was nowhere to be found.

I woke up one morning, and I couldn't even get out of bed. I had absolutely no energy. I couldn't go to school. It got worse, and my father just left me for days on end by myself. I couldn't eat anything, and there was only apple juice so I sipped on water from a jug I filled up. I had to crawl to the kitchen sink and back.

One day, he came home with a different woman, who thankfully insisted my father take me to a doctor immediately. I would tell Doctor M. but he wasn't listening. He told me I had strep throat and sent me home. He brought me home, and for the next two weeks, I was left by myself, getting sicker and sicker. I would hear the phone ring, but I couldn't answer it. I could only crawl to the bathroom and to the kitchen to get water.

As I was getting weaker my jaw wouldn't and couldn't open any bigger than for the tip of my tongue to stick out. I would sleep on the couch because it was central to the bathroom and kitchen. After two weeks of this, my friends started getting concerned and came over to check on me. One of them crawled through the living room window and then let the others in through the front door that she unlocked.

My father had never once called the school or even my swim coach. I think my friends were horrified when they saw me; I had dropped weight and I couldn't even stand up when they walked over to me, lying on the couch. They most definitely told their parents when they got home because my father showed up shortly after that.

He HAD to take me to the hospital now. But, he didn't. He didn't because two years before, I was admitted for some unknown sickness. My mother took me. Then she left me there after the doctor insisted I be checked in for a few days. My father came that night and yanked me out of bed with the nurse behind him insisting I stay. He took me out but had to bring me to the ER because I couldn't stop throwing up after he insisted I drink a bottle of ginger ale. To this day, I remember a doctor telling him that if I wound up in the ER again, he would call the police and let them sort it out.

So, nope, no ER, but he took me across from Saint Charles Hospital to a doctors center. The woman at the desk saw me and immediately called the doctor while putting me in a wheelchair. She took me into a room and helped me onto the table. The doctor appeared right away.

I was sitting/lying on the edge of the papered table when he opened the door. I was wheezing and had trouble even swallowing my own saliva.

"Oh my God," came out of his mouth. Then he felt my throat and asked me to open my mouth. I couldn't. That's when this kind and big muscular doctor put my face in his hands and said, "Sweetie, I'm not going to lie to you. This is going to hurt, but I have to do this." He took my jaws, forcing my mouth open. The reason I couldn't open my mouth was because there had been an internal abscess where my jaw connected. I didn't scream, but tears poured down my face. Then he told me he had to feel inside my throat. He had rubber gloves on and felt inside my throat. My wheezing was due to the fact that my throat had almost swollen shut!

The doctor immediately laid me down, with the nurse helping him by getting a needle ready. He explained he had to drain my throat immediately, and so he did. He told me I was incredibly brave. Then he asked me why I didn't go to the doctor sooner? I told him the truth. That my father left me alone for several weeks and how my friends came by earlier to check on me. That sent him marching out to see my father who was out in the hallway.

I heard the doctor's voice, then some arguing because my father was an arrogant asshole to people when he was threatened. But this doctor wasn't scared of my father's threats in fact he yelled at him, telling my father that one more night I would have choked to death in my sleep. I looked at the nurse who was in the room with me the entire time. She must have been a mom because she came over to ask if she could hug me, and I let her.

I went home. The story would be that I had mononucleosis. I would return to school fifty pounds lighter and I was not an overweight kid to begin with. There were audible gasps and looks of sympathy from my teachers. I would go to school for the morning return home at lunchtime, and then go to school the next day at lunchtime to take my afternoon classes. I had missed over a month of school altogether! I think my teachers felt sorry for me. I caught up quickly, except for math.

By the time I turned 17, my father and his patsy of a girlfriend were getting married. She was too stupid to see his act. I believe he married her because (A), she was stupid and (B), to get access to her beautifully towheaded three-year-old granddaughter. (I wouldn't put that last part together for over twenty years.)

She also had her own business of taking care of elderly able-walking women in her own home, and was getting five hundred dollars a month from each woman. I would get an invitation to have dinner with her and my father but the real reason was for me to watch the old ladies while they went out to dinner and a movie and such. She wasn't a drinker nor a partier. She was a perfect patsy, with all the religious bullshit included.

One day, I saw paperwork for an annulment from my mother on the dining room table, so my father could marry the patsy in the catholic church. Under some section, he had written how my mother was pregnant. and that's why they got married. As horrible of a woman she was, I never did believe that. But the best part? The stupid woman, the stepmother-to-be, had been married seven (7) times and was seven (7) different religions, and now here she was becoming catholic to marry him! They got married in the church after she took the required classes, and she never attended a catholic service after that. She didn't do anything sporty with him later either. These two deserved each other.

Back with Mother and Brother

I couldn't stand the way she treated me, couldn't live with them and moved back in with my mother and brother. My brother couldn't stand the stupid woman either.

But being out of that house for a few years changed things! Not for the better. Our beautiful house was now filled with dog shit from their two dogs. Every dish was filthy in the sink, and every bit of space was covered with dirty dishes and trash. My room was filled to the ceiling with garbage bags. In every room were stacks of stuff. It was an awful, disgusting mess! My brother lived in this mess, not lifting a finger to do anything. I was completely shocked, and instantly depressed.

I began cleaning up the kitchen. On that day, I had been washing dishes by hand for a few hours because the dishwasher was broken. My brother walked in and punched me so hard on my left shoulder, I almost fell over. I was washing a large knife, and at that moment with one swift move, as he turned to leave the kitchen, I threw that knife as hard as I could, barely missing his head and sticking into the swinging door. He slowly turned around and looked at me in shock. Before he could say a word, I simply said in a very calm voice, "If you EVER touch me again, I will cut your throat from ear to ear while you are sleeping." He would never punch nor touch me again. As an adult, I realized something in me could only take so much.

As much as I tried to clean the house, my mother and brother didn't do any cleaning at all. I was too embarrassed to have anyone over. Our house smelled so bad. I'd come home, and my mother would be watching TV with dog crap everywhere. I was always the one to clean. We had a dog kennel, along with a fenced-in back yard. Our beautiful home with beautiful furniture was ruined. I would believe we were the only people living like that until the show HOARDERS came out, years later. To this day, I have only seen commercials for it and I cannot watch it.

Graduated High School

I graduated high school. If a counselor had shown any interest in me, I would have gone to college. I had no idea about the SATs. There were no sit-down dinners when I was growing up. There was no talk about the future for me. All I knew was that I kept telling myself I would get away from these crazy people.

Every night no matter where I was, I told myself I would get away. By the time I was eighteen years old, I had had my fill of disfunction and crazy people. Between my mother, father and step-monster - I had to escape. Right after I graduated, I went down to the recruiters station. I talked to the Navy recruiter on my own. I never told a soul what I was doing. I would study for the ASVAB test away from my house, keeping my book hidden. I just wanted to get out and away from Bend. Away from the looks and whispers. Away from the crazy people. I wanted no association with the people who raised me. Just away from it all. Little did I realize how fucked up emotionally and traumatized I truly was.

THE NAVY- June 1985 – 18 Years Old

I joined the Navy without an A (advanced or technical training) school. At the time, I had no idea that I could have my choice of A schools. I performed very well on the ASVAB test. Nor did I know my recruiter had so many undesignated spots that he had to fill. It was June of 1985. I had to wait until September 14th. That was the soonest the Navy could take me in. So, I was living back with my father and step-monster; I had to quit my job and get one closer to their house because I didn't have a car.

I worked at a place called *Speedy Mart*. The owner's name was Mickey, and I really enjoyed working for her. My father was a chauvinistic, arrogant man among other things. So for me to be working for a woman was inspiring. *Speedy Mart* was a gas station and little market. I worked every shift I could just to stay out of the house. I also had to stay away from any bad influences because I would be taking a urinalysis for illegal drugs to enter bootcamp.

Back in 1985 in Oregon there were no self-service gas stations, by law. I got to pump the gas and check the oil level when asked to. At 18, I could sell beer and wine; I just couldn't drink it. I really liked that job because my boss trusted me to let me work on my own. Two weeks before I was headed for bootcamp, I told Micky that I was leaving for the Navy. She was really bummed out about that. Around that time, I mentioned to my father that I was leaving for bootcamp soon. The thing he did next would stick in my memory for my lifetime.

In 1985, it was illegal to join the armed forces if you were a homosexual. My recruiter called me because he needed me to sign one more paper at his office. A friend of mine drove me down, and there on his desk was a paper and a pen. I read it, and then I signed it. I looked up at my recruiter, a bit confused. You see that paper I signed stated that I WAS NOT a homosexual. Then my recruiter said, "Wow, your dad doesn't want you leaving."

I answered him with, "That piece of shit has never been my dad or a father to me; I was adopted at birth, and he can fuck off."

With that, my recruiter said, "Now that makes sense." He chuckled and then told me I would do just fine in the Navy. That paper I had to sign? That would come up in therapy years later. He tried everything for my recruiter to not accept me, even to make up a story that I was gay.

The night of September 13th, I was so excited to get the hell out of there. Little did I realize at that time how much help I would need for my emotional issues. I just wanted to get away. I never got into any serious trouble growing up, knowing my father would never help me. My brother always got into trouble, and my father always got him out. In fact, my brother was convicted of drunk driving, nearly killing a young woman, and spent only a few months in jail for it.

On the 14th of September, 1985, I took a cab down to the Trailways Bus Station and waited to board. I wouldn't feel freedom until I was on the plane in Portland and headed for Orlando, Florida.

Freedom in the Navy

I had to make it through bootcamp because I had

nowhere else to go. Bootcamp was easy for me. The yelling in my face I never took personally because I certainly wasn't being called a cunt or bastard, etcetera. Eventually, I had to get up earlier than the rest of company 138 to teach the girls who didn't pass swimming and help them pass their swim test. Being around water all my life, I was curious as to why these four girls couldn't swim, so I asked them. They grew up in the city with no access to lakes or rivers, and the swimming pool cost money. I got all four of them to pass their tests.

One day, I got called out to talk to one of my company commanders asking something about letters from my father. I was so embarrassed, but I told her he wasn't my father. That I was adopted and getting away. She told me that, after the first letter, she just threw the others away because how he described me was nothing that she could see. I think she understood more than I did at that moment, and for that I am forever grateful.

I only had one problem in bootcamp. My right boot didn't fit correctly, and I was too scared to complain because I didn't want to be held back. A calcium deposit had formed below my big toe and would hit a nerve.

Thankfully, I could tie my boots just right that I was ok during the day. It was at night when the pain came. I had taken my boots off and was kind of rocking back and forth when one of the girls near my bunk could see I was in pain. She asked if I was ok. Then told me it was okay to cry. After that, the girls covered for me if needed.

We had a Master At Arms that was a bit of a tattletale, and one night when I got up to use the bathroom, she was asleep in her top bunk. Thankfully no one was underneath her, because she wet the bed. I covered for her not telling a soul, but only after we made a deal that she would stop being a tattletale on people. As I write this, I wonder what trauma she was running from. I hope she got the help she needed.

Eight weeks in bootcamp and I graduated. I still had no clue about an A school. I had to stay in Orlando and take a basic class on different aircrafts with a few other girls from my company. It went quickly and we graduated from that. I got my orders that I was going to San Diego. But first, I would have two weeks off before I reported for duty. I had no place to go, and the navy already bought my tickets back to Bend and then on to San Diego.

It was Christmas Eve, and I had nowhere to go, so I flew to Portland and then hopped on a tiny plane to Redmond. There I took a cab to my father's law office and crawled in through a window. I found out they were in Las Vegas. I stayed at his office at night and would go over to a friend's house during the day. She was home from college for her Christmas break. On January 9th, I was on my way to San Diego. I was nervous. When I got to Coronado, it was almost midnight, and I checked in at the nick of time.

Coronado - 1986

The next morning, I got to see what the base looked like. It was January 10th 1986, and I felt like the luckiest 18-year-old alive! I was stationed on North Island at HS-10. The HS-10 Taskmasters. If you have ever been to San Diego and look at the Coronado Bay Bridge, to the side you will see North Island and two hangar bays that were used for blimps at one time. We were farthest from the water. It was the most beautiful sight to me: the San Diego Bay, the Coronado Bay Bridge, downtown San Diego across the bay, and helicopters coming and going.

I was first assigned to the Line Shack, which was located on the side of the tarmac. We didn't call them helicopters or helos. We called them aircraft and by their number.

Each aircraft had a large number printed on both sides. I was never one to just sit around so I immediately asked what I could do? I didn't realize at the time that (A) I was beautiful and (B) I liked to work. I fit right in, and I liked it. I would go on to become an Aircraft Electrician by studying a friend's workbooks from his A school, and I would make rate.

I loved being in the Navy. I felt safe at my command and on base. My only mistake was getting married. I really don't have much to say about that. He was incredibly handsome, and I went home with him one night, and he insisted I stay. Years later in therapy, I would come to understand that his insistence was more of a command, and no wonder that I didn't have the language to stand up for myself. My childhood trauma had a lot to do with that.

I was happy for a while. I loved how neat and tidy and clean Luther was. We didn't even wear shoes in the house. A habit I keep to this day. But things got bad when we both got switched to night shift. He would drink nine to twelve beers before we even left for work at 3pm. He was a controlled alcoholic. I just didn't know it yet.

Then one night when we returned from a party, he got angry with me because he thought I was flirting. He took my right hand and squeezed it so hard I was on my knees, begging him to stop. He broke seven bones in my hand and broke my wrist. The next morning was a Saturday. I got dressed and went over to Balboa Hospital ER. I lied about what happened. Of course I lied; I was scared, and still brainwashed about lying about abuse. They put a cast on and gave me plenty of chances to tell the truth. I couldn't.

Monday morning came around, and I'm in my commands main building walking to the maintenance office when I heard my name being called. I knew that deep voice well. That was our Flight Surgeon. I pretended not to hear him and went out the side door. He went out another door and caught me. He took me aside and explained how, as our HS-10 Flight Surgeon, he sees all the medical files of anyone in our command that goes to the ER.

In a very serious tone, he told me that if my husband did this once, he will continue until the abuse gets so bad he winds up killing me in a drunken rage. I had been seeing our Flight Surgeon for over a year on a weekly basis because I had fallen off a parked aircraft. I messed up my shoulder and neck, and I was back and forth to Balboa until they finally did the surgery. I should get disability for that injury that I still suffer from, but the hospital lost all my records! I only have what they gave me.

Anyway, I left my husband, but not after he wiped out

our joint account! I got out of the Navy in September 1989. When I look back, I think I was afraid of my ex-husband and really tired of my medical issues.

Post Navy – September 1989 – 1994

I would have jobs here and there, but I had no direction. I was seeing someone that none of my friends liked there in San Diego. I had nobody in my life ever, to give me advice. I'm not proud of the fact that I had a few years of hanging out, drinking and drugging with the wrong people. One of those people would do his drug dealing business in his garage with his garage door wide open. I'd often sit off to the side, sipping a beer and watching the tv he had in there. He had a pool table so people would hang out. Not just buy and go.

Eventually as I was sitting there one afternoon, I noticed an old white moving van that hadn't moved in over a week. Then I noticed that the empty house across the street had an upstairs window with curtains on it that would move. I pointed this out to my friend, who just said I was being paranoid. A few nights later, the van had moved to where it had a clear view of my friend's garage. I pointed that out to him, and he just laughed. I got a beer and as I opened it, I heard that familiar calming sweet voice firmly say my name and LEAVE NOW! I put the beer down gently, waved goodbye, got into my car, and left.

Not long after that night, I heard the news that my other friend got busted by the DEA. I was right about the van, the window curtains of the house across the street, and that it could mean bad news. I was so scared. I really didn't know anything about his drug business. I had only helped him with his legit roofing business. I decided to pack up my car and leave for Washington State where I had friends, and I could figure out what I was going to do with my life at 27 years old. While in Washington, I found out I was pregnant by the boyfriend none of my friends liked. His name was Clay.

1994 - Baby Days

I had to call my now ex-boyfriend Clay and tell him I was pregnant. He convinced me to come to San Diego, CA. He had his own business; an art gallery. He said that he didn't want me working while I was pregnant.

"Who is going to hire a pregnant woman?" He convinced me. I utilized my time by going to the library and learning what I needed to know about pregnancy. I had sold my car in order to fly back to San Diego. I didn't have health insurance, so once a week, I spent an hour on the bus going to the clinic and an hour back. Each week, I was given a urinalysis. I thought it was routine. The truth was they were only checking for drugs in my system, although I didn't realize it then.

Toward the end of my pregnancy, I would tell the doctor (who quite frankly didn't care) how thirsty I was. It was an unquenchable thirst. My boyfriend Clay would have nothing to do with me. He would leave early for work and come home late in the evening. I could feel his resentment towards me, and nothing I did changed that. I asked him one time why he even wanted me to come back. It would take me years and serious therapy to realize it was all about his own ego. He was a forty-nine-year-old man, who wanted to look virile by having a kid. He had been embezzled, over $100 grand; and was married and divorced three times by the age of forty-eight. He would lie to me for years about the reason his first wife left him with their child, and she had all contact cut off until she was eighteen years old.

I was miserable. I didn't want the baby to feel that way, so I stayed busy. I played lots of different music, and I talked to the baby all the time. I kept Clay's place clean. I always made dinner for him. But it was clear that Clay didn't give a damn about me. I suspected he was seeing another woman. I was right, but I never told him I knew. I will come back to that. I should also mention that he was twenty-two years older than me. Our relationship started with a lie. He told me he was divorced when actually his divorce wasn't final for another six months when we had started seeing each other. I was young, stupid, and thought I loved this man. What did I know about love or a healthy relationship? What did they look and feel like? I didn't have any women mentors. I had absolutely no loving family either. I only had my friends that were my age. No wonder I made the choices that I did.

I gave birth to a healthy baby boy at nine pounds and seven ounces. Afterwards, I would find out that my unquenchable thirst was actually gestational diabetes. Let me be clear that it's important to mention that Clay did not take me or attend even one doctor's appointment. It didn't even concern him how thirsty I was either.

Thankfully, our baby boy didn't have gestational diabetes, and I no longer had it shortly after he was born. So, you probably know how after the mom gives birth, typically the nurse gives the baby to the new mom. Clay took the baby from the nurse before I had a chance to hold him! I remember the surprised look on the nurse's face. She said no father had ever done that before, took the baby out of his arms, and gave him to me. (That move would be brought up in therapy years later).

When asked why he took the baby, he stated he wanted HIS son to connect and smell him FIRST! Now, let me explain that a little more. When Clay bought a beautiful chocolate Labrador while we were dating, I made a dog bed out of a box and put one of my old sweatshirts in it for comfort and warmth for the puppy. That dog, Jake, loved me and followed me everywhere. It would be later that I read that partly due to my sweatshirt, the scent of me created a connection. So Clay wanted that when our son was born.

Clay turned 50, eight days after our son was born.

Suddenly Clay wanted to be a dad, on his own terms of course. He would feed him while I was sleeping if I pumped a bottle of breast milk, but he NEVER changed a diaper. He would *never* clean up puke or anything a baby does. I had such love for our baby that it never grossed me out. That first moment and every time after, I would look at my son and wonder how on earth anyone could hurt a baby or child! I threw away all the books that told me to let my baby cry and self-soothe. I followed my heart and loved every moment of having this precious baby boy in my life. He was half of me and the happiest baby.

When our son was a couple months old, Clay's daughter from his first marriage wanted to meet her baby brother. I was thrilled she wanted to meet her baby brother. I was twenty-eight and she was twenty-four.

Just hours before she landed, Clay handed me a ring. There was no marriage proposal. There was no I love you. It was simply, "Here, put this on, and one day we might get married." I didn't put it on. I walked into the bathroom, turned the shower on, and cried into a towel so he couldn't see or hear me. I wanted to take my baby and run away from this man! I had nowhere to run to! I had no one to help me!

So I gathered myself, washed my face, and walked out of the bathroom. He insisted I put the ring on. So I did. I wanted to go to the airport with our son to greet his daughter, but he angrily told me no. When he returned with her, she was such a lovely sight. Her energy was beautiful, and the way she connected with our son made me happy. Even though there was a twenty-four year age difference, I wanted her to always have a relationship with her baby brother. She was real and honest. She commented on my ring, asking how her dad proposed. I was too embarrassed and ashamed to tell her the truth. I would tell her a lie that I would tell anyone who asked how he proposed for years. I would say he left a note in the garden that we had out in front of our house. He went along with that lie.

When our son was nine months old, Clay suggested we get our marriage license. I was such a fool because as I was doing the paperwork, he found a female judge and said, "Why wait, let's do it now." I asked him if he had married any of his other wives that same month. He lied and said no. I didn't learn about this lie until years later.

After we were married, he said he was holding an opening at his art gallery, and we needed to make an appearance. This art gallery was in downtown San Diego. Walking in first holding our son, he told everyone we got married, and his son was his best man. He never held my hand or even looked at me. I was feeling absolutely alone. A little while later, I was listening to people having a good time and commenting on our baby in the other room. That's when I heard my new husband tell his friends with a chuckle, "Yeah, I figured since I bought all this food, I would marry her at the courthouse and this could be our reception too. Plus, the young ones are easy to train."

I just sat there in the dark, in the art display room, ready to cry and so angry with myself. None of my friends liked him - they had warned me that he was a selfish asshole.

At least my first husband Luther and I had a wedding followed by two weeks in Hawaii. Clay and I never had a honeymoon. What he claimed as our honeymoon was a working vacation for him, where we brought the baby along.

Second Ex-Wife

Our son had turned one year old when I answered the home phone one afternoon. It was a woman who wanted to talk to Clay. I explained he wasn't home. This is when I found out about his second wife. He never told me about her. I gave her his personal number at work. She said she just wanted him to sign off on a piece of property. I could tell in her voice she did not like him. She was all business. When he got home, I asked him about her. He got mad at me for asking, so I dropped the subject.

I loved being a mom. I would hold my beautiful baby boy and could never imagine ever hurting him. I never let him cry himself to sleep. I remember one day looking up at Clay to say, "We have it pretty easy with him." He was a happy, curious and smiling baby. I thought I was happy. I had no clue I was in a completely dysfunctional, controlling marriage. I really wanted a "normal" life.

Baby #2- 31- 1998

Three years later, we had another pregnancy. He was fifty-three and thrilled about it. I was thirty-one and scared! This time, I had insurance and it was suggested that I be induced to avoid getting gestational diabetes again. We had just finished remodeling a Craftsman-style house near Balboa Park before our beautiful baby girl was born. She was beautiful!! I was really happy with my babies and Clay was happy to have a little family of his own.

My happiness surrounded the babies. They were my priority. I told Clay he had to get a vasectomy. He said he wanted to have a few more babies. I flat-out refused. I loved that we had a boy and a girl. I felt like he wanted to control me by having several babies to keep me tethered at home. No time for me to have friends. He could have friends to do whatever whenever he wanted. Thankfully, he wasn't too much of a night person, and it seemed to me that he loved coming home to the kids.

Right before our daughter was born, he bought an old building that he wanted to restore in a tiny, and I mean tiny, town on Highway 395 in the middle of nowhereI didn't want to leave San Diego. I didn't want to leave our beautiful, restored home, so close to the park. Why did he want us to leave? He had two art galleries that were finally doing well making life simple to manage. I was not a high-maintenance wife. My life was about our children, our family. We could afford for me to stay home. We both agreed that we did not want our kids growing up in daycare.

Where are We? Middle of Nowhere.

Our daughter was six months old when he moved us. He got to be the big man in town coming from San Diego who bought three pieces of property in a town that had a population of 500 people. He would spend two and a half years working on a building that was over a hundred years old. Every two weeks he would leave us in this town, where I knew no one, to go check on his galleries in San Diego and Coronado for a week.

Our house was only a few blocks away from the renovated building, and one night, our baby girl was crying, probably because she was teething, and since Clay wasn't home yet, I put the baby in the car along with my son and drove around until they both fell asleep. When I pulled up to the house, I noticed he still wasn't home so I turned the car around and drove over to the building and walked in the back door.

My husband was with a woman I did not know! They

were having a glass of wine and laughing! I left without him knowing that I was there. By the time he got home, I asked him why he was working so late. He got mad at me, so I retreated. After being married almost three years, he was not wearing his wedding ring that I bought him for our one-year anniversary. I insisted he wear it but he didn't. I hated living in that town.

The women were mean, jealous, and judgmental. They thought I was a spoiled rich, young, housewife when that wasn't the case at all. I was married to a man who flirted *right in front of me* with women in town. I was married to a man who would never tell me how much money he made or tell me his social security number. I was never allowed to be on his bank account nor have my own bank account. He controlled all the money. He controlled everything. became incredibly depressed.

Depressed

I wasn't even allowed to give him any suggestions I had for the building. For instance, when he was almost finished with its renovations, I suggested tiny white lights in the trees in the garden area. He got angry with me, so I left. One week later, I walked up there with the kids to find that he was sitting with a woman I didn't know when he said, "She has the best idea, white lights in the trees in the garden." I just left without argument. This would go on our entire marriage! I would give him an idea, and he would either take full credit for it, or shoot it down and then give another woman the credit if she gave him the same idea.

I fell into a deep depression living there. He never noticed or cared. He was all about his own ego. I would not see that truth for many years to come. I was so miserable I didn't want to be married to him anymore. We got into a heated argument when out of nowhere he slapped me HARD! He had never been violent towards me before, and it shocked me.

Then I got angry enough to look at him and say, "If you EVER hit me again, it better be hard enough that I never get up again because I WILL fucking KILL YOU!" I took an angry step forward, looking him straight in the eyes when he stepped back. He knew I meant it. He had never seen me angry like that before. I lived with violence my entire childhood and with part of my first marriage. I was not going to repeat that.

I went into the house to see my face in the mirror. I called the police immediately and had him arrested. He only spent one night in jail; the charges were dropped because I didn't have the courage to follow through. He would lie to anyone listening that he didn't hit me. But my neighbor saw my face. She was one of the few nice older respected women of that town. Clay despised her because she was a strong, independent woman. I liked her because of that. When she saw my face, I was embarrassed.

She just simply said, "Keep adding lots of salt to his food, Honey." Then she gave me a little grin. She believed me, which meant the world to me! Today, I believe she saw exactly who he was. With a twenty-two-year age difference, that's a flashing warning red banner, not just a red flag!

It gets worse

Clay wanted to take our kids away from me, claiming I was unfit to anyone who would listen, and called his friends from San Diego, asking them to write letters on his behalf. He would call his last ex-wife to come testify on his behalf. The worst part? Clay had the audacity to call my adoptive father and stepmother to testify against me. They drove down from Oregon completely on his side. It would take years of therapy to realize that my father wanted my young children around for his own sickness. In the end, my husband's mother put a stop to it by driving to the hearing where she refused to testify on her son's behalf. She had been around me with the babies and told me many times what a wonderful and patient mother I was.

It would also be a few years before I would find out that the local district attorney's investigator was the one who put a stop to everything by one simple act. When my father and his wife showed up and spoke to him for their written statements, he was absolutely appalled (but did not show it) that a father who was an attorney himself would do what he did to his daughter. When their written statements were finished, he took them. He never gave those statements to anyone; he simply put them in his desk. We had never met officially; he often saw me with my children around town and at the restaurant, and he being a good judge of character, knew everything my father wrote were lies, horrible lies.

Despite all this, Clay still got my precious babies. He took the kids, went to the hotel we owned and cleaned out the bank account. I had no one to help me get my children back.

I give up – you win – I lose

I am ashamed to say I gave up. My life was nothing without my babies. I had no one to turn to for help. I walked to the local minimart, bought a six-pack of beer and 4 bottles of sleeping pills. My husband had taken my kids out of pure spite. I took all four bottles of pills, with about three and a half bottles of beer, and then I wrote a letter to my young children. I told them how much I loved them. I told them how sorry I was for leaving them. I told them how alone I felt in this world. I told them how their Grandmother, the only one I considered their Grandmother, was the only one who stood by me and treated me with kindness and respect.

I'm not sure who called the ambulance or who found me. I don't know how long I was out. The next thing I remember was loud banging and being put into an ambulance. The nearest hospital was about fifteen miles away. I remember some discussion of a fire. Apparently, the ambulance engine had caught on fire, and the driver refused to stop, saying that I would not live if he didn't get me to that hospital. That driver was my husband's nemesis by saving my life by not stopping until we arrived at the hospital. I would find out later that people who witnessed the ambulance arriving were shocked it actually made it. The flames were raging.

The next thing I remember was a nurse talking to me. I couldn't open my eyes or speak since I was in a coma, but it was the kindness in this woman's voice I will never forget. Then, she began to cry a little. Those tears were for me and my two little kids. She spoke directly to me, telling me I was beautiful and to just hang on. That life would get better. I could feel her put the Vaseline on my lips and wipe them a bit. I had tubes down my throat. I couldn't move or speak.

I'm not sure how much longer or even days later while in a coma that the white haired, bright blue-eyed man showed up. He was in the bed next to me, sitting on the edge facing me. I cannot remember exactly what he said to me or how long he spoke. It was his calm demeanor and voice that somehow gave me the will to live. "It's time to wake up."

"It's time to wake up."

He stayed with me until I woke up. I remember a beeping alarm followed by the nurses and doctor coming into my room. They took the tube out of my throat so I could breathe on my own. As I was taking in my surroundings, I got a bit confused because there wasn't a bed next to me or a man with white hair and brilliant blue eyes.

My first words to the doctor and nurses were, "Where is the man that was on the bed next to me? Where is the bed?" In my confusion and slow to comprehend my surroundings, they sent a woman to evaluate me. I guess I didn't answer her questions correctly because the next thing I know, I am being carted off to Century City in an ambulance a couple hundred miles away. But before I was loaded into the ambulance, a nurse told me that no one had been in my room, that there wasn't even enough room for another bed. I recognized her voice. She was the kind nurse who took care of me and spoke to me when I was in my coma.

Century City is in Los Angeles. When we arrived, I saw the tall buildings without any clue where I was going. The EMTs wheeled me in on the gurney to the elevator, where we stopped on the top floor. When the elevator doors opened, I was pushed into the hallway and left there for about a minute. On my left was a large wooden door with a square window at the top and several curious faces trying to look out the window at me. I turned my head to my right, and there was a similar wooden door with a square window at the top and a few smiling faces. My only thought was, "Please let this be the door I go into." I was still pretty sedated, thankfully. My biggest fear came true, I was in a looney bin! To my relief, the EMTs wheeled me into the right-hand side door.

I was wheeled into a very large pink room. A gross pink. Gratefully, I had it to myself with a nice view of the city and the busy street below. I was switched from the gurney over to the bed, and the EMTs left. I fell back to sleep.

Every four hours, they woke me up to take my vitals and to draw blood. I never said a word. I just let the nurses do their job. In the morning, I got out of bed, dressed in the clothes that someone had given the EMTs. There were nice women from the town in the middle of nowhere who came out of the woodwork to send clothes with everything they thought I needed. They also made sure my children were ok with their father too. My first morning in Century City, I heard what would be the morning announcement:

"Line up for your meds, please."

The staff at Century City were nice and kind. The facility was always clean with bright lights during the day. I was given a pamphlet to read, and I read it. (I would be thankful I did.) The first few days, I just walked around to take in my surroundings. We couldn't leave the floor, which meant that technically we were locked in. There were group meetings we had to attend a few times a day. I didn't talk at these meetings. I rarely talked at all. One day after our last meeting of the day, the counselor pulled me aside and asked me why I was there. I told her, I tried to kill myself and that I came very close to succeeding. She told me flat out that I was not like anyone else on that floor. That I would figure things out because I was smart and observant. I stood there dumbfounded. She smiled. I could feel her honesty.

I walked around the facility a lot. Eventually, I would meet a man who first introduced himself as John. Later that day, he would introduce himself as Juan, in a Columbian accent. One night when I was walking the hallway, I would come across Juan. He was mumbling in Spanish; I could see he was sleepwalking and stressed. I pulled up a chair, and in a soft but firm voice, I told Juan to sit. He sat down immediately. I could see he was doing something with his hands. I watched him without a word. A staff member came walking down the hallway, so I explained to them that Juan was sleepwalking, working through some things, and we shouldn't wake him. She pulled up a chair and together we watched in silence. We could see he was "assembling" his "gun."

When he was through, he got up and went into his room. "How did you know he was sleepwalking"? The staff member asked me. I told her that I sleepwalk when I am stressed out and that my first husband was a Vietnam veteran with horrible nightmares. He too, would assemble his imaginary gun.

It's possible that after that interaction, the staff could see

I wasn't going to be any problem, so they let me do what I wanted. One evening a bit late, I could hear someone was being checked in, so I peeked out my door to see what was going on. The man on the gurney had been there before because the staff knew him. I could tell they liked him. The next morning I walked by this man's room when I heard him call out to me, "Hey you, come here please."

"No." I said and kept walking. I heard him chuckle. Later on I walked by his room; this time I paused and looked in.

We made eye contact, and then he asked if he could talk to me. He asked me what his condition was when he arrived the night before. I told him he was a bit out of it but weren't we all when we got here? Then he told me he tried ending it by jumping in front of a semi-truck.

I replied with, "Well your aim was off because you missed!" I said it in a dry tone surprising myself that my dark sense of humor just came out to a total stranger. He laughed hard at that, which made me smile. Then he asked me what I had done to be there. I smiled and asked if it was a contest. We became fast friends. He was nice to me, and never inappropriate towards me in any way, shape, or form, which I appreciated. We both had a dark sense of humor that made life better there in the Century City psych ward. He was a writer for a very popular show at the time, and people were obsessed with it. I had never watched the show but had heard about it. It was before streaming came along when tv was where most entertainment came from. That absolutely thrilled him that I didn't watch the show and that all I knew about it was through tv commercials.

We got bored one day, so we started a game called, "name that attempt." We would watch out the window of a person being unloaded from an ambulance to guess why they were sent there. The two of us would then discreetly wait by the door as the new patient arrived. Then we would meet up in the group room to discuss our answers with each other. Most of the time, he was correct but it was our interactions that were so much fun. We were never mean to anyone and always befriended the newcomers. Slowly, more and more people joined the game. We had only two rules: be kind and never embarrass the arriving patients. John (Juan) also became our friend and would ask every morning if Juan was around the night before. It was interesting that John respected the fact that I, a woman, had served in the U.S. Navy.

Eventually, there were a few women who joined the game. We became a "welcoming" committee! Then THAT turned into a group meeting where most everyone knew about the game, and for some unknown reason, it set an interesting vibe in the place. People started socializing a bit more. More people attended the group meetings with the counselor. There was a little bit of laughter around there.

There was one man who was in another room; it was pink and padded. I was told that he never spoke. He never attended group meetings since his meds were brought to him. There was a window for the nurses to check on him when the door was closed. We could see him as we walked the halls. He was never mentioned in our game because that would have been cruel. I and my writer buddy were not cruel, nor were any of the patients there.

One day for some reason, I stopped at his door to look in. He was sitting on the padded floor against the wall staring. So I asked the staff if it was okay for me to sit with him with the door kept open. They said it was ok. So I sat with him never saying a word; he didn't either. I sat with him every day after that. I think he felt lonely. There was a certain comfort in sitting with him in silence.

One day, my writer buddy got bored, so we made up a new game. We were convinced the door across the hall from us held the more mentally troubled people. Just like us, if you wanted to go outside, there were specific times the staff would take a small group out for about 15 minutes to smoke or just be outside. My writer buddy and I turned it into, "Who's gonna run?" My room had the perfect view of the street to see what was going on around a busy city bus stop. This game became popular quickly and it was fun! We were not hurting anyone, and no one from the street could see us at the window. We would watch body language, point things out, and discuss if that person was going to run. My absolute favorite winner was one that my buddy called it.

There was a very tall man in a hospital gown and slippers, puffing away on his cigarette. My buddy kept saying, "See how he's looking around, like for a taxi or something? I figured the man was antsy, like most of us. But low and behold, my buddy was right! The next thing we know, as the people were gathering to go back upstairs led by a staff member, our man in the gown was last in line, suddenly flicked his cigarette and ran for the city bus!

The bet was now on and a bunch of us were yelling in my room if he was going to catch it or not! He did, and he was gone. One of the staff members came in to see what we were making noise about. We told her while we were cracking up, I mean the man's gown was flapping while he ran which exposed his very white butt. You just can't make that stuff up! The staff member immediately got on her radio to talk to someone from that ward. The man was returned to his ward within the hour.

Keeping busy was imperative or I would go crazy, was my daily thought. I started to tell myself I was just resting from life. I could see that other people had a lot harder time with things, so when those people laughed, me and my buddy were happy. There were visiting hours. Family members would show up to visit. My husband never did, nor did he call to check in on me. I missed my children terribly every day but kept that to myself.

One evening, I was told over the loudspeaker that I had a call. The phone was in the hallway; I picked it up thinking it was my husband. Now this next part, I've never told anyone. I said, "Hello?" and the next thing I hear is my father's voice laughing, telling me I'm a "hard one to kill."

My eyes welled up from hurt and anger as John walked by. He could see that I was upset and asked if I was ok. I just handed him the receiver and walked away. John listened and surprisingly, John said into the phone, "You worthless piece of shit! I should hunt you down and gut you like a fish!" I turned around with my mouth open. John hung up the phone. When he walked over to me, he told me I was a beautiful soul on this earth, that no man has the right to talk or treat me badly. I thanked him for that. A little while later, the men and women who played our game came over to my room to check on me. There was so much kindness from all those people that I have never forgotten.

So much kindness.

Sometimes, when family members came to the hospital, they misidentified me for a staff member. I would usually direct them to where they needed to go. By the way, I told them I was a patient. At first, the looks they gave me were embarrassing so then my writer buddy made it into something humorous. He could always make me laugh.

Eventually, it was time for me to leave. There was a woman who showed up carrying files and looking a bit disheveled. She went into our group meeting room and then called my name in a rude tone. I'll admit I was a bit thrown off by her rude attitude towards me. I got used to the Century City staff being nice to me. The woman flipped through what looked like my file and then slammed it shut. She informed me she would be advising the staff that I would be here for at least two more weeks, maybe a month, until it was time for another reevaluation.

Now, remember that pamphlet I was given on my first day? Well, I had read it and kept it. In that pamphlet, it explained how I had the right to be seen by a judge within the next 24 hours. I sat there and looked at this woman in silence. There wasn't a reason to keep me, and I knew it. I also knew I had to stay calm and not overreact. So, I very calmly and quietly said,

"I'd like to see a Judge because I read the pamphlet I was given, and I kept it." With that, she took a big breath and smiled at me. Then she told me I was ready to go home. Somehow, I passed her test of possibly getting angry and overreacting. I would find out later that my husband was pushing for me to be committed. If I had overreacted that day, things might have turned out differently. You see, in that same pamphlet, I read that I had the right to see a judge, a staff member would have to take me on a bus, and stay with me for the entire procedure. That is not something I imagine they enjoy doing.

"I'd like to see a Judge."

That counselor of our group meetings caught up to me later and told me I did a great job requesting a Judge, reaffirming that I didn't belong there. She advised me to get therapy, and if I did, I would see in me what she saw in me and that I would be ok.

I sat once more with the quiet man in the pink-padded room. It was the only time I ever spoke to him. I spoke softly and thanked him for letting me sit with him every day. I told him I was leaving, would not be back because I needed to take care of my little children, and that I missed them terribly. I got up, touching his shoulder lightly. As I turned to go out the door, he quietly and barely audibly said,

"Thank you." I never told anyone he spoke until writing this book. I figured he had his reasons for not speaking, and I respect that.

I gathered my things because one of those women from my town was picking me up to drive me home. I was surprised it was her because I didn't think she liked me. Yet, the kindness and understanding in her eyes said everything to me.

I said goodbye to my writer buddy, who in turn told everyone I was leaving. I had made friends with a bunch of strangers who wished me well and told me not to come back, all in love! I often wonder about my writer buddy. To this day, I have not watched the popular show he wrote for. I like to keep him safe in my thoughts the way I remember him. I'd like to think he's living a happy, peaceful life. I am happy he is still alive, according to the internet.

Middle of Nowhere with my Babies

I would return back to the town in the middle of nowhere to be with my babies again! Someone set me up with a psychiatrist that I would have to drive 45 miles each way to see once a week. He was a bored old man who was way past retirement. I was not comfortable with him. There were no female shrinks in the area or even female therapists at that time. I had good insurance, which is all that mattered to the old man. He sent me home with several prescriptions. On my own, I found a support group. I was welcomed there by some nice people. The support group was in the same town as the old man psychiatrist 45 miles away from mine. Just when I started to feel a bit better, Clay told me I was needed at home and that I would no longer attend those support group meetings.

I couldn't fight him.

I couldn't fight him. He could of course enjoy the Jeep he bought himself to go explore the desert. He could enjoy and feed the horse he bought himself too. I had no one. He spoke to his mother on the phone early in the morning every day. I began shrinking back into my shell. The only thing that made me happy were my two young children. Since returning, I would tell them every day that I loved them! One day, Clay got angry, telling me to stop because it wouldn't mean anything to them. He could never bully me enough to stop! Never! I was grateful I was alive to watch my children grow up! I love them dearly!

I never explained to him why I did it.

I knew I had to get out of that desert town; I was pushing him to do so. I believe my mother-in-law was instrumental in that push too. I wanted to go back to San Diego, but he didn't. He kept insisting we couldn't afford to go back, but I knew he was hiding something from me. I just can't put my finger on it. He got very angry with me, so I would stop pushing for San Diego. Then I decided on Reno since his mother and stepfather lived about an hour north of there. They would be close by and they loved their grand babies, which I was thankful for.

We sold his restaurant in the middle of nowhere to a couple who had young school-age kids. The husband traveled for work so the restaurant was for his wife to run. We sold his motel too. I was never allowed to know how much money was made or see any of the books. I only use the term WE because my name was included on the papers. Technically, we were still in escrow with the restaurant when we moved to Reno, Nevada.

Reno, Nevada

We had a big old house. It was bigger than we were used to. It needed work but, that was all cosmetic. I believe we had only lived in Reno for no more than two weeks when the phone rang in the middle of the night. The restaurant had a fire, and it was too far gone to save.

Within an hour, Clay was on his way to go see the damage, not even waiting for daylight. It was a four-hour drive in the middle of winter.

Someone with a video camera filmed the restaurant burning in the dark of night and gave a copy to Clay which he brought back to Reno to show to me. I wasn't upset it burned down. Yes, I felt bad for Clay because I wasn't a heartless woman.

When the restaurant burned to the ground, the last thing to burn was the beautiful statue of a Native American that stood at the front entrance as if he was holding the building up. Clay purchased it on a road trip in the middle of nowhere at a vintage store, maybe because of my reaction; I fell in love with it immediately. He was not a sentimental business man, which makes me feel sure he purchased in part to look good to the nearby Reservation that the local Paiute Natives lived on.

That restaurant was over 100 years old and twice before whatever stood before, burned to the ground too. We were in a Native country, and I am part Native. What I never told my husband or anyone else for that matter, was that I did see the spirits of Natives all around and throughout the building and its property during the time we lived there.

Years later my daughter would speak about a woman who would make little bracelets with her out in the garden area of the restaurant. I never let my children go unsupervised. I remember my daughter at four years old out in the garden making those bracelets, but there never was a woman with her that I saw making those bracelets. She would describe a Native woman. I believed her. I was not meant to see that Spirit; she was for my daughter only.

Because we were still in escrow, I insisted we keep the insurance until the sale was final. He actually listened to me because there were other people there who agreed it was the smart thing to do.

The kids and I were happy in Reno. We had lovely, nice neighbors, and the kids had lots of friends. Clay in the meantime became incredibly grouchy towards me. He would contact a friend of his that had a gallery on Maui to fly over for a couple of weeks at a time. Just as we were settling into Reno, Clay convinced me to move to Maui by flying me and the kids out there during their Spring Break from school. He would tell the kids it was for me, and maybe it partly was. I came to find out Clay would take our insurance money and "buy" his friend's gallery there on Front Street in Lahaina. It was a scam. His so-called friend knew he was losing his lease in the year we were there. Clay clearly told him about our insurance money.

A Gallery on Maui

Summertime came, and Clay took one more trip to Maui before we all moved there. He had been very busy working the gallery. While he was gone, the phone rang one night around 10pm. I let the answering machine pick it up. It was Clay's last ex-wife. I quickly picked up the phone so as not to wake up the kids. They were too young for them to know about all of Clay's ex-wives.

She had been drinking and wanted to get it off her chest about the affair she had with Clay while I was pregnant with our son. I didn't want to believe her. But in my heart, I knew. I think I actually knew when she had given a baby gift after our son was born, and a staff member told me who it was from, yet Clay lied about it. I told her we could talk another time. After we hung up, she called the local police to check up on me. She was concerned for my safety. That would stick in my head for years. "My safety?"

I had compassion for her and I am thankful for that because my children overheard me speaking to her and they remembered that years later and told me so. They even remembered the police showing up and how I handled that.

We lived three blocks from the gallery, and three more blocks from there was the kids' school. After school, both kids participated in the swim team. Life was simple. I loved Lahaina. Every Sunday, we spent on Baby Beach with another family. One day, I noticed a car following me and the kids. I'm pretty good about taking in my surroundings without being obvious. I didn't say anything to my husband until the third day it happened. That's when I told him about the car. He told me it was a small island, and I was just paranoid. I believe it was the sixth or seventh day of being followed that it happened. Turns out it was my husband's latest ex-wife! She had flown out from San Diego and was stalking me and the kids!

She finally walked into the gallery. I believe all these years later that the only reason he told me she had shown up was because his employees liked me, and he knew someone would tell me. I always had a bit of compassion for her. She had become a full-fledged alcoholic. I believed it was partly from not having closure from their marriage and affair afterward. Throughout the years, she would call while in a drunken episode. Before cell phones, it was on our home phone. I was always polite to her.

When my husband told me she had shown up to the gallery, I asked him how did she know we had moved to Hawaii, let alone Maui, and zoned in on Lahaina? He of course got angry, so I wouldn't ask any more questions. I think he wanted me to be jealous of his ex, but I never was. She was beautiful. I'll bet that, like me, she was never told that either. He clearly had a type.

I couldn't figure out for years exactly what kind of person I was married to.

His jealousy over things I could do or experience I had was just plain immature. One time, he put a basketball hoop up and challenged me to a game of HORSE. I easily beat him. He never knew I played basketball! He would NEVER play basketball with me again.

Teenagers in Capitola, CA

Life went on, and the kids were growing up. We finally settled in Capitola, CA, because his elderly mother and stepfather had been living on his stepsister's property in Hollister, CA, just over Mount Madonna from us. They didn't want to live there anymore, so they bought a mobile home in a nice, safe mobile home park not far from us.

I had made a promise to my mother-in-law years before for her intervention with my husband trying to take my kids away from me. I promised I would never put her in a home, and I kept that promise. They lived in their place for about a year when my father-in-law died. After that, my husband would go see her most mornings, and either me or one of our now teenage kids would go over in the evening to take her a prepared meal. She had spent years making every meal for her and her husband.

We found out that she rather enjoyed a certain brand of frozen dinners. She was not one to be fussed over. We also took her shopping every Tuesday. A few times a week, my husband would take her to work with him for the day. He was out of the gallery business and now into Mid-Century and vintage furniture. It looked good having his ninety-year-old little American Sicilian mother at the store in her own chair reading and chatting with customers. But my mother-in-law was there for her own reason, which I loved her for. She was keeping an eye on her son. She would tell him when she thought I was not within hearing her, "Your wife comes first, Clay." Clay loved to flirt with the beautiful women and always allowed women to flirt with him right in front of me. His ego wanted to make me jealous.

Recently, a dear friend and I were talking about jealousy. I didn't understand it, but am comfortable enough with close girlfriends to admit if I am a tad envious of something. I told her I thought jealousy was an immaturity of one's soul and spirit. She responded with, "Girls compete with each other and women empower each other." In my own head, I added that husbands can behave like jackasses!

Working with my husband didn't last long. Every suggestion, every movement of an item, no matter how small, made him angry, which I was tired of. I also started having a few glasses of wine every night.

Cage Free Big Dogs

Not long after, I landed a great job. One of his customers came in to have her furniture loaded that she had purchased the night before. She had her pickup truck with a Doberman Pincher in the cab. She didn't know who I was, and I just happened to be out in the parking lot because I was visiting a friend nearby. I walked over to her truck while she was in the building. The window was down, and the dog was sitting behind the wheel. He was cute, and I started talking to him.

I could see he wasn't dangerous by his actions, and I'm sure my energy let him know I wasn't either. While I was petting him on the head, his owner came out and was stunned. She said, "I can't believe he is allowing you to pet him!" I told her I had always been good with dogs since I was young. I laughed and told her how I was the kid who fed all the dogs in my neighborhood in the summertime when families or retired people left on vacation. Right there, she asked me if I wanted a job. She told me to call her the next day and gave me her cell number. I did, and she asked me to come to her place, giving me the address.

It was out in the country near Watsonville. She was on a few acres of land she had purchased the year before and had just started a cage free big dog boarding business. There was a security gate that had rubber buttons. It was easy to figure out the code of 1234 by looking at the wear pattern. She laughed and was impressed when I arrived at the 2nd gate fifteen minutes early. I was greeted first by the biggest dog I had ever seen! I'd been around plenty of dogs in my lifetime. Behind him was the woman walking over to greet me.

Kato, the English Mastiff (now simply called mastiffs) was apparently a test. A few other people who saw him never came through the gate! I laughed because I could see he was just a big ol love. He weighed close to 200 pounds! He was a retired show dog who I loved immediately! Slobber and all.

I loved this job that lasted a few years. I loved having my own money even though it mostly went to food and whatever else Clay insisted I pay for. I think my boss figured out what kind of man I was married to because she would give me cash tips and tell me it was for me and only me. Being around different breeds of dogs and outside in the country suited me very well. I kept things very clean, and every dog got attention.

In the afternoons, I would take my lunch break and read a book with the dogs lying around me. It was peaceful. Those dogs taught me a lot about my own energy. I was always kind to the dogs. It was not my job to train dogs. But there were days I would show up rattled from something Clay said or did. It was clear the dogs could feel it. I had to learn to just let it go before I walked through the gates in the mornings. The dogs made me happy. I didn't have to talk to the owners. I just wasn't sociable enough to do so. That was my boss' job. I got to work on my own because my boss trusted me enough to be on my own for the day.

If she wasn't back when I was leaving for the day, her husband would have been. We got very popular; people started noticing that their dogs would get excited on their return trip about a mile away from the farm. When they arrived, the dogs would jump out, excited to be back. That was great for business.

Then came the day that Clay insisted that I see a

therapist he found for me. Found? His method was asking every woman who came into the store what their job was, and whenever it was therapy, he would ask for a card for his wife.

We separated for 6 months, and he took the kids since he had the money and power and made life hard for me. I was back home when he informed me that he had made an appointment for me and if I didn't see her, he would divorce me. I actually pondered that in my head for a minute in silence, knowing that I would get no financial support from him. So I agreed. I asked my boss if I could come in early the next day and told her why. She told me no problem, to come at my normal time, and she would still pay me for eight hours. I was thankful for that.

Linda

Therapy. I had tried on my own over the years, and it was always male therapists on my insurance. Never any women. I was nervous going into that first appointment with her. I showed up early and quietly opened the door to the lobby. There were three doors, two of which were closed; I could see the name plates, so the third door that was open clearly was the woman I had to see.

Now picture this, her door was wide open, and a woman with very long silver hair was sitting in a chair in the middle of her office with her back to me. She had no idea I was there. When I want to be very quiet, I can be. That skill was from when I was a kid and had to sneak to get food in the middle of the night. I don't barge through doors or things like that, and sometimes I just want to scope out a new scene, so I am quiet.

I sat in the lobby not making a sound, and then she walked out. She had a look of surprise and said, "Oh, you ARE here." I replied with, " For about ten minutes now." I told her how I didn't want to disturb her because I was early. She introduced herself as Linda, and she invited me into her office. I looked around in silence and liked how there were no personal photos. That there weren't knickknacks cluttering her office. No stupid sayings telling me to hang on, or to give myself a pat on the back. There was a large window too, that looked out into the big trees and the creek below.

It was also very quiet. I liked that. I looked at her Mid-Century furniture, and with a straight face I said, "You have good taste in furniture." She chuckled. I sat down on the couch in front of her. I wasn't happy being forced to see her. I didn't trust that she was friends with Clay, and I told her so. I sat not taking my eyes off her. In my mind, she wouldn't want me as a client within three visits.

That's when Linda explained to me she and Clay were not friends. She had done business with him, and as charming as he was with her, she knew a salesman when she saw one. My mind actually raced, but outwardly, I remained calm. I didn't trust people, especially if they were Clay's friends. She asked what the age difference was between us and then sat in silence with me.

I relaxed just a bit to feel what I always called privately in my head "The energy." Then I realized she was gay. She was beautiful, and Clay had no idea she was gay! That made me grin. She knew I figured that out, and she smiled back at me. I instantly went back to being serious. She respected that. She asked me why I thought he wanted me in therapy. I told her I probably changed a bit after someone I loved and respected died the year before. Then we sat in silence. She didn't force me to talk. I didn't want to show my emotions for my dead friend Drew. He was my Navy Flight Surgeon who stayed in touch with me. My eyes started to bubble up, so I looked out the window. I hadn't spoken about him since his "death."

My first session ended, and she softly asked me if I would like to come back for another session. I told her I had to. Clay threatened to divorce me if I didn't. She gave me a little smile of sympathy, and I looked away. I didn't want her pity. We agreed that I would see her the following Tuesday.

I went to work the next day and told my boss I would be seeing her again, and that's when my boss said the strangest thing to me, "You're gonna get better and then leave me!" I looked at her perplexed and went to feed the dogs. But what she had said would stay with me.

The next session, Linda brought up Drew's name. I told her I wasn't ready to talk about him. That as a kid I had lost two friends, and I was told by my parents that people die and to get over it. That I hadn't really learned to deal with death growing up so, I guess I just stuffed it down and left it there. She then asked me about therapy and if I ever had it before. I told her my experiences and that my last try was while living in Maui.

That the shrink was from the Mainland, which bummed me out. Worse yet, I told her was, "That fucker fell asleep within the first five minutes of both sessions." She asked me, "Both?" I told her I only went twice. That second time he fell asleep I wrote on a yellow post it, "Fuck you, I am not paying for this," and then I stuck it on his bald head that was face down on his desk and walked out."

Linda started chuckling, then caught herself seeing that I was serious. I looked away and said, "I suppose it is funny." Then I looked back at her and gave her a little grin. That's when she suggested that he might have had narcolepsy. Then I told her flat out that I don't trust people. That I never had anyone to trust. That I didn't ever trust Clay. As a child, I grew up with my adoptive parents, especially my father telling everyone who mattered that, "I told little stories." "That I was a liar." Linda got very serious and asked me if I ever told Clay that. I told her no. I told her how when I told Clay that my adoptive father abused me as a child that, I instantly felt energy from Clay that he thought I was lying.

Then shortly later he hired my father, who had retired from law supposedly, to work on a project with Clay. I explained that my own husband could give a shit what I think and what I feel. That every time things were going well, I fell for it. And every fucking time, he yanked the rug out from me. I no longer fall for it. It's like his sick game. That I have come to despise the game he plays of being the "oh so loving husband" to strangers and has my own kids question me and my sanity.

My anger then grew into a controlled rage. My voice was low and monotone. "When Drew died, that night when Clay came home, I had been crying, and in his annoyed tone, Clay asked what the matter was. "Drew died." I told her how Clay literally said, "Oh" in a I don't give a shit voice. I told her I had known Drew long before meeting Clay, and Clay was always jealous for no reason. But how

Clay flirts with every pretty woman right in front of me. I then sat in silence, realizing how much anger I had for Clay. " He only said "Oh" and walked into the fucking bathroom, and he's supposed to be my husband." I said that out loud and not really to Linda. We sat in silence. Then quietly, Linda said, "Tonight I want you to ask Clay if your father ever told him, "you told little stories."

That night when Clay got home, I asked him that question. He looked at me nonchalantly and said, "Yeah, he told me those exact words when I met him for the first time." I looked at him in disbelief and said, "And you never thought to tell me that?" I didn't wait for his answer. I was so incredibly hurt that I left the room, but not before saying, " I've never told you anything deep about myself because I learned from the beginning of this so-called marriage that you wouldn't believe me."

I believe at that very moment it occurred to me that Clay really NEVER cared about me. I hated how he let my adoptive father and his stupid wife into our lives but, I think I hated myself more for not putting my foot down, until I finally did. I continued to tell Linda how angry I got at Clay because he was still talking to them and reading the letters he continued to send. I got so fucking angry that he wouldn't tell me about the letters. I'm thence who always looks like the crazy one, I told Linda.

The following week at my appointment, I told Linda what Clay's response was. I had a habit of sitting in silence, and she let me. That was the week we officially started doing the therapy I came for. It was called Eye Movement Desensitization and Reprocessing Therapy. E.M.D.R. for short. I had never heard of it, but it was fairly new, and Linda was one of the few therapists in town that practiced it. It was so much better than talk therapy alone, for me. I finally felt like this was going to be okay. That EMDR was going to help me.

One day out of nowhere, I started humming a song softly to myself. I was at home after a long day at work. The kids weren't home yet, and Clay was still at work. The song I was humming was strangely familiar but I couldn't say what the name of it was. I wasn't known for humming either. I think this was the point where that veil of lies began slowly lifting in my life. Therapy had begun working. I liked Linda, and I liked having a woman as my therapist. Linda was ten years older than me and had some life experiences that connected us.

That tune kept coming into my head??? It's "This Little Light of Mine." I probably had heard it throughout my life and just blocked it out so I really didn't HEAR it. In therapy, I once mentioned that I had blanks in my memory. Yet I had such detail for so many things but then big blanks. I told Linda I couldn't really explain it. That's when she told me, "It's how our brains protect us until we are ready for the truth." I stared at her for a minute, really letting that sink in. It was almost like hearing a riddle that I would have the answer to one day. It stuck in my brain, and that veil continued to lift.

EMDR therapy really helped me. In the beginning, she had me come in twice a week when things got a bit heavy for me. I don't know about you, but it's weird that an hour of therapy is only fifty minutes, but I was always ready to get out of that room. In my mind, I was actually compartmentalizing. I was leaving everything that was brought up in her office there until the next session.

My marriage wasn't getting any better. He was never home until late, and I stopped waiting for him at dinner. I began isolating myself and having my few glasses of wine in my bedroom, which eventually turned into a bottle of wine. It was the only thing I felt I had control of. He controlled every aspect of the marriage, but to the world, he was a loving and concerned husband. Who was he to tell me I couldn't drink? When I say control, I mean things like, he would never let me know how much money he earned, and I wasn't allowed to ask without an argument. He would have so many irons in the fire for distraction. Always stressing me out on what needs to be paid, yet buying a car for himself whenever he wanted to.

As for cars? Clay was going to buy our daughter another car when she actually stopped him from doing so, expressing to him how I had been driving the same car for fourteen years. She was right. Both the kids had a few different cars, and Clay had too many to keep count. That was yet another veil being lifted. As I am writing these words, I am so grateful that both my kids are kind, thoughtful human beings.

I was in therapy for about a year and doing better mentally when I began standing up to Clay. You see, when the kids were growing up, they saw their mom putting on an act when it came to their father. He was always teasing me, and I fucking hated it. I had been teased ruthlessly as a child by both my adopted parents, especially by my father in front of other people. So for my own husband to do it to me in front of our children upset me. I didn't want to fight in front of the kids. For example, he always teased me about being in the Navy. That the Navy was full of gays on ships, everything was gay, and that I was probably gay.

The reality that I would find out years later? He would tell the story of how he quit the Air Force because he objected to the Vietnam War. The truth was, he was kicked out on an *other than honorable discharge*. Also, he was drafted into the Air Force. He willingly joined the Air Force because he was drafted.

As I progressed in therapy, I began questioning him on a lot of things, and he would stay at work later and later. He wasn't really working; he was drinking, and some of these people he was drinking with were other women. I drove the mile down to his business one evening, and there he was sitting with a beautiful woman and no one else, drinking and laughing away. I stopped making dinner for him that night. When he got home, I asked him where he had been and he got angry, as usual. The next day, he informed me he would no longer be paying for my therapy because "WE" couldn't afford it. "WE?" I asked. "You have never included me in anything, and now it's "WE?"

My next therapy session, I told her what had happened and I would need some time to come up with the money. (She didn't take insurance). I would also have to cut it down to one session a week. Within a few months, I had saved enough money and had a budget so I could afford therapy, and then I was back on track. I was really healing as I discovered my marriage wasn't a marriage at all. I mean, let's face it, twenty-two year age difference was mostly for his ego but he sure made me feel like I was the screwed-up one.

I came to understand that when I married Clay, part of me felt safe. Since I had been molested much of my youth, there was one thing I sexually didn't like doing. My first husband understood that with love and compassion, and Clay didn't like it. So this is why I felt I was going to be safe with Clay. That he would protect me and keep me safe. I thought I knew about love, but I didn't even know how to love myself, so how on earth would I expect to be loved with respect and honor?

Therapy just kept slowly giving me answers that I myself would figure out with my EMDR tools. I also had to sneak to therapy. Sneak to therapy? How ridiculous is that? I couldn't tell Clay I was back in therapy, or I knew he would require me to pay for things he could easily pay for. I wasn't a high-maintenance wife either. I didn't have credit cards; I didn't get my hair done weekly or my nails. I didn't go out with friends. The problem was still my unhappiness, and I dealt with it by drinking in my bedroom after work. It hurt, isolating from my kids, and feeling like the third wheel in the family. I loved my kids so much and their father was always entwined in their lives making sure he was never left out. He would tell the kids lies about me that I still don't defend. I know they will figure them out eventually, just like I finally figured out who I was married to.

One day, Linda blurted it out, and it was probably about the fourth or fifth time, but that day it sunk in. She said, "You DO know you are beautiful, right?" That last time lifted that veil even more so. It occurred to me that here I was married for over twenty years, and he had never told me so. In fact, the beauty of my children comes from me, I realized! Not only their hearts but their looks! The friends I have would always tell me that both my kids looked like me. The only thing my son had of his fathers was the cleft in his chin.

My friends would also say that Clay was lucky to have such a beautiful woman who was his wife. These things from past and present really started to sink in. I mean what kind of man doesn't tell his beautiful wife she's beautiful? What kind of man never buys his wife an anniversary present? What kind of man never buys his wife a birthday present or even a card? What kind of man drinks at his business after hours with women who throw themselves at him? What kind of man controls the marriage never allowing his wife to be a partner? What kind of man portrays himself to strangers as a caring husband but never to his wife? What kind of man ruthlessly teases his wife harmfully in front of his own children?

That kind of man? I will get to that later.

Therapy continued, and it wasn't always easy; I was always trying to better myself. My brain felt so scrambled when it came to my childhood, and thus the reason I didn't like to talk about it. I had these blocks in my brain, and sometimes when things began to surface, I wasn't prepared for them. Then sometimes, things would surface, and it was as if I was embarrassed for how I was treated as a child. I would eventually figure out why I felt that way.

Then there was the time I described in detail an abusive situation that happened to me when I was about five years old. When I looked over at Linda, I saw tears well up in her eyes and I looked away as if I didn't notice. She quietly got up and excused herself. I stared out the window at the hummingbird that was close by. I stared at the trees and just let my mind drift until she returned a few minutes later. Linda sat down and asked me to look at her. That's when she told me in the fifteen years she had been a therapist, she had never had a client that was as abused as I was; with the coping skills I had. I was immediately embarrassed; I didn't want her pity. It was a defense mechanism that I learned from an early age because as a kid, *no one's pity was enough to help me*. Then my controlled rage started coming to the surface; I needed to get out of that office.

I know when that controlled rage starts to show itself because the tone of my voice changes. I don't yell. It's more of a deep, methodical tone. I once had a friend tell me, "I'm glad you never get mad at me because you scare the shit out of me when you are angry." I didn't really hear what she meant at that time because it wasn't something I was proud of. As crazy as it sounds, I was never allowed to get angry growing up. But I also knew that the anger I had and the dead-eye look I'd give without blinking was my power. It was the only power I had. There were times in my marriage I used it towards Clay as my last resort because that was the only thing that would stop him. Then he would try and guilt trip me later.

The next session with Linda was when she asked about that rage. I told her why I had to get out of there. That, as crazy as it sounded, I could feel her pity, her sadness, and I didn't like it, and it wasn't just the tears I pretended not to notice. That's when she asked me if I was told, "Stop being so sensitive" as a kid. I told her yes, and even my husband said that to me. Linda just stared at me for a moment. Like she was forming a question in her head. Then her demeanor relaxed and she half smiled. "Now we are getting somewhere" she said. She would explain to me what an H.S.P. was and told me to do some homework on it. Nothing too deep. Just to go online and look because things might make sense to me. We did some EMDR after that, and I went home and drank in my room, which happened more as I got into the deep stuff in therapy.

The veil was lifting.

One day on my way to therapy, and this is hard to explain, but I would always mutter something of protection for me when I needed it throughout my life. Again, the veil was lifting and things were bubbling to the surface. So when I got to Linda's office as usual, I had a serious look on my face. I mean, in retrospect, I was taking therapy seriously because I wanted to get better. When I sat down, she looked at me strangely and had me go into EMDR immediately. I would hold these two pulsating handles, one in each hand, with my eyes closed. I discussed what came up, and it was just too much, too quickly, and I opened my eyes.

Linda asked if I was okay and I shook my head yes. Then I took a deep breath, and I felt the calmness that came with feeling that sense of protection when I needed it. But I didn't say anything, and I didn't let that show outwardly. I let my few deep breaths out slowly and then I looked at Linda. She was as white as a ghost and, I don't know why but out of my mouth I quietly said, "They protect me when I ask them to."

Linda asked me softly if I believed in angels. I told her I didn't like talking about that subject because I am not religious. To me, religion had shown me nothing but hypocrisy, and I believe angels exist but they are spiritual. She wrote down the name of a book for me to read by Lorna Byrne, "Angels In My Hair" Although her experiences are different, she made me feel like I wasn't crazy. After reading her book, that familiar humming happened more and more. Then one day, I would come to realize the song was "This Little Light of Mine." I would come to realize why I had stopped singing it and humming as a child.

My drinking would continue, sometimes after a hard therapy session and mostly when I was in my bedroom after work. I had always been able to stop when I needed to. But I didn't feel the need to stop. Then, I made a stupid decision on a Friday night that turned out to be something good in disguise. Something that I needed.

I would get a DUI leaving a business party at Clay's

business. I was angry at his flirtatious behavior towards one woman in particular that was obvious to me they had something going on. I drank so much that I was in a blackout and woke up in jail. My daughter came to get me because Clay refused to answer his phone. I was completely humiliated, but I would need that to stop drinking.

On Monday when I went in to see Linda, she insisted I go to an AA meeting. I told her no, and she said if I didn't go, she wouldn't continue helping me. So she sent me to a large meeting where I could blend in. She knew I didn't like attention drawn to me. I think I groaned outwardly because she kind of chuckled. I hadn't had a drink since my arrest, and I had no desire for one either.

The next day, I walked into the AA meeting Linda insisted I go to. I had on a hoodie and a ball cap pulled down to my eyes. I didn't want anyone to look at me. I was filled with shame, but the room was filled with people smiling and talking amongst each other. I introduced myself as a new person and followed the directions when the secretary asked if anyone was in their first thirty days of sobriety. I didn't know what in the hell I was doing, but the energy was really nice in that room. I began going every day and sitting next to the same two people. I was then told about an upcoming dance that some guys from AA were playing at with their band and encouraged, not pressured, to attend. It was the first dance I attended alone and without a drop of alcohol in me since I was a kid. Alone and without at least a serious buzz? Who was I?

I would slowly find out who I was by attending meetings and listening. The woman I sat next to almost every day and had coffee with occasionally, in my fifth month of sobriety, wound up taking her own life. I walked into the AA meeting that Monday and sat down to a very solemn row of people. One of the women I had slowly interacted with walked over to me and quietly told me about it before the meeting started. I was so shocked but held my demeanor and got up and walked outside. I had been around death growing up. I had a few classmates murdered and few who died from accidents. Out of that sadness of losing a sobriety sister came the gift of the most amazing three women that I absolutely enjoy, love, and respect to this day.

Therapy along with Alcoholics Anonymous really began

helping me put the pieces of my life together, past and present. After I got my DUI and attended my first AA meeting, Clay left me. For the first time, I wasn't worried about how I was going to survive. I felt a sense of freedom. The way he left me was pretty shitty. He had our daughter summon me downstairs and while he sat in the corner behind her, he had our daughter tell me he was leaving me. I simply shrugged my shoulders and replied, "Okay." and walked back upstairs. I will admit, later I was angry he put our daughter in the middle of that while he sat behind her. But that's who he is.

A Sense of Freedom

I was doing really well, and he couldn't stand that so, he kicked me out of our place. I had no idea I had the right to stay there since I was on the lease. He had controlled every aspect of our "so-called marriage." But my AA friends found me a place to live. Then that ended when my housemate relapsed, but I then found another place. I never worried. It never entered my mind. I stayed away from Clay, but he would pop up places he knew I would be at with another woman, and I didn't care. I was slowly learning who I was and more about who he was, and he couldn't get under my skin like he had done successfully in the past. I simply didn't care, and that felt wonderful!

Therapy was going great, and then the hammer came down. Linda, being my therapist for a few years, began behaving differently towards me. Her energy was weird. Some days, she would be overly nice, crack jokes, and give me gifts and then other days, she would be very serious and demanding. After a few times of this happening, especially the over-niceness, I became leery of her and began reading her energy before every session. I began feeling that I couldn't trust her, and that's when she insisted on giving me a hug as I would leave my sessions.

What she didn't know was, I knew that hugs were a form of manipulation and control. Then it happened. I walked into a session, and she was very formal. Unlike she had ever been around me before. That's when she informed me she wanted to write a book about me. I didn't really hear much after that as she rambled on. My brain was spinning. How could she do this to me? I'm not a fucking circus act! My controlled rage started to bubble up, and then I heard her say, "You will have to sign papers from my attorney that he has already prepared." I was getting angrier by the minute as she went on and on. Something about my coping skills and how I was an HSP and protective angels and blah blah blah when out of my mouth came, "STOP TALKING"!

I got up, and I walked out the door. I drove my car to the beach and got out. My rage was palpable - I had to walk or run or do something! How could she do this to me? I trusted her! I told her things I had never told another soul! My life was so fucked up, she can make money off me?!

Was it all bullshit?!

I was incredibly angry, hurt, and my mind was spinning. Then I began feeling how she had probably discussed me amongst her friends. Keeping the confidentiality by leaving out my name. I would walk until I was calm, and then got into my car and drove home.

The next day, I went to my AA meeting, sat in silence and rage, not speaking to anyone. It was clear I needed to be left alone. In the passing months, I had become sociable in those meetings and realized people liked me. So there were no nosy questions, just a few people telling me if I needed to talk, they would listen. I appreciated their kindness but passed on that. As I sat there in my silent rage, the only thing I heard was, "If you didn't drink yesterday or before this meeting, you did good." I may not have listened to the speaker that particular day, but I definitely heard what I needed that day. I didn't drink the day before when all that had happened.

My rage lifted to just highly upset. I went home and blocked the therapist's number. I opened my email, and without reading the therapist's email, I deleted and blocked her. I found out where she lived and dumped every stupid manipulative gift off, (by the way, a therapist should not be giving gifts to their clients, I found out), on her driveway. I knew better than to knock on her door because I was angry. I would see her in public a few times, and she would immediately turn around in a hurry, when I would give her my blank stare. I definitely used my anger energy to keep her away from me, and she clearly felt it.

I would eventually get another therapist and on my first session flat out said, "If you know or are friends with Linda, this won't work." I knew she was telling me the truth when she said no.

Moving On and Getting Clear

I had stopped drinking going on five years ago and was in therapy with my new therapist Jillian for a couple years and feeling better emotionally. Life was life, but I was handling it. Clay and I were divorced. After two children and twenty-five years of marriage, he walked away scott-free. I would not see any financial support whatsoever from him.

Here is some of who he is: I had married a liar, a cheater, and a master manipulator who once again, ran away from his responsibility. What did I expect? He didn't pay child support to his first child from his first marriage. He didn't pay any alimony to any of his wives. In fact, our so-called marriage began with a lie. I had asked him if he had married any of his first three wives the same month we got married, the week we got married. He brushed me off with a curt, NO! I found out that the truth was: his last wife and he WERE married the same month we were. They were the 2nd of the month, and we were the 20th.

So, at this stage of therapy and sobriety, the pieces of

my life just started falling into place. I was sitting in Jillian's office when *I realized I had married my father* and I physically... felt sick. The only differences were that Clay wasn't a pedophile or murderer. But in every other sense, he was *exactly the same*. He was controlling. He was a cheater, a liar, and a manipulator. He made me feel crazy when I wasn't crazy. He gaslit me and he was jealous of any friends I had and usually chased them away by being a completely rude jerk to them. Oh, the list goes on, but you get the point.

The pieces continued to fit into place. The following session, I sat there in silence understanding *the narcissist that I had been married to.*

After more therapy and processing, I decided that I wanted our grown children to have one last Christmas with both parents, a nice dinner together. Clay was getting close to eighty years old, and I knew I could show kindness, for my grown kids. Things went well, and my kids were happy and I was polite.

It was the following day when Clay came over that he started showing me a statue and told me how much he paid for it. Then he told me about trips he had taken. All this without ever even offering me 20 bucks for gas after our divorce. Remember, I get nothing in support. I let him go on and on, and then he tells me about how he's got this girlfriend who used to be gay for years and years but how they get together because she wants a man now, and there are no strings attached. It's just lots and lots of sex with no commitment. Oh, and how they are leaving tomorrow to fly to Arizona for the New Year. I didn't say much. I think I didn't say anything. I just listened and watched this pathetic old man that I didn't even recognize because I was seeing for the first time who he really was, very clearly.

The comment about her being gay and wanting a man now? That comment came because he would always say that me and my best friend were gay and gay for each other in front of my young kids. It would always bother me in the past, but *on that day I saw how insecure he was.* My grown children know the truth. The comment about lots of sex is when I saw who he REALLY was. *He was a man who has never known true intimacy and actually has no respect for women at all.* Our sex life was only about him. He would get angry and make my life hell for a few days if I denied him sex. When he was finished with sex, he would roll over to his side of the bed. Sex was all about what he wanted only and when HE wanted it. I never, even once, had an organism with him.

What I now saw, was a twelve-year-old entitled little boy whose parents had a successful, popular restaurant and bar in a little town where everyone knew who little Clay and his family were, including extended family. It had all been taken away without warning and with complete humiliation. The marriage ended due to the father's alcoholism. Clay's mother took him and his brothers to her mother's house. There, they would stay with their Grandmother for several weeks in San Jose, CA, while their mother was in Nevada. The boys had no idea what was going on, and they had no idea where their father was. When Clay's mother returned from Reno, Nevada, she was divorced from Clay's father and was now married to a man who had worked in the restaurant for Clay's father. At twelve years old, Clay was in a new town. He was the new kid in a new school. The life he knew was forever gone. That twelve-year-old Clay, never grew up emotionally and was forever stuck in this now old man's body.

Clay never knew how to be truly intimate and never

will. He tried his best that day to upset me. He could upset me in the past, but it will never happen again.

That day in Jillian's office was revealing to me because I also realized it bugs him to no end that I have not relapsed since I quit drinking. In fact, early on in my recovery, one of my children was overheard saying something to the likes of, me being fine without him and how maybe my drinking had a lot to do with him. I'll be honest; that makes me smile. I'm human. I also realized he was actually trying to get me so upset that I would relapse that last day or soon after. In the end, I don't blame Clay for my drinking and he's certainly not worth a relapse!

I now understood his not wanting me to continue my support group years ago and the therapy he stopped paying for. It *was because I would see who he REALLY was.* I would gain strength and control of my own life. I was married to a narcissist manipulator who used me, and had to control me, because that was the only kind of woman he could get. Women his own age and who came from a good foundation with healthy self-esteem, wanted nothing to do with a man like him. *Men like Clay are predators.* They go on the hunt looking for the beautiful women with low self-esteem issues. They only want a woman they can control and use.

Forgiveness?

With Jillian, I learned that forgiveness isn't really about the other person at all. It's about letting go and moving forward. Top that with a dash of AA, and it's not letting the past ruminate in my brain like a damn hamster wheel round and around for my entire life.

After that last encounter with Clay, I told my kids that I needed boundaries when it came to Clay. I told them I would always be there for my kids if they needed help concerning their father.. They know I'm not angry, and they understand completely. The one thing I have done as their mother is to let them have their own relationship with their father. I do not bad mouth their father. They are smart, observant, and I expect that they will figure out the truth on their own.

After those revealing sessions and acceptance, (and that took time) with moving forward, therapy REALLY opened the door. I just had to see it, be brave, and walk through it... to my freedom.

To be honest, I am not a big AA thumper. But, if I had not stopped drinking, I would still be miserable with the blanks in my memories that alcohol would only numb but never resolve. I would still be angry just below the surface. I would still be resentful.

What I didn't realize with Linda, my first EMDR therapist, was that those memories that were bubbling up to the surface and my drinking after those sessions just pushed them back down. I was on an emotional see-saw and had no clue. But with Jillian and a few years of EMDR therapy along with learning about WHY I drank, in AA I was ready to be free and live the life I deserved.

Sitting in her office on that particular day, well I certainly didn't expect what would happen in that session! That was the day Jillian asked me a few questions. I answered her, and then it began.

Those puzzle pieces turned into the game, Plinko. You know, the game on *The Price is Right*. The contestant would put a piece at the top and it would bounce around side to side and finally end at the bottom with a money prize. I'm talking Bob Barker era, by the way. Well that's how it happened. Jillian's questions were at the top, and I sat there as the answers mentally bounced side to side when out of my mouth, I piped up with, "Holy Sh.." I didn't even finish cursing. In fact, with therapy, I wasn't as angry, so my cursing dwindled down to a slow drip and not a sailor's mouth. There I sat in silence with answers coming in full force, and thank goodness my therapist did not interrupt me. Finally, I looked up at her and said, "They sold me." "The cars, the houses," I continued to name things off. More to myself and not to Jillian.

"The drugs and alcohol they forced on me." "The strange men taking me away."

"That bedroom that was picture perfect, yet I wasn't allowed to touch the fancy dolls on the shelves!" "Oh my gawd, the PINK carpet, and fancy dresses!" "The Polaroid camera and the home 8mm camera!" "That day my mother went berserk....dressing me like a boy and chopping all my beautiful hair off!" Those were only a few of the things I had said out loud. I would drive home in silence from that session. It's really hard to put into words how I felt that day.

Over the next few months, my Plinko had turned into a thousand-piece puzzle that started off with muted colors. I took the answers from my therapy sessions, making those the corners and then the frame. Slowly putting the pieces together until the picture that was my childhood had been completed. Those last few pieces in the middle were hard. To know that my adoptive parents tried to kill me. That moving to Bend, they figured I wouldn't remember, and when I did, they tried again to kill me. The constant making me feel crazy by being told I was a liar over and over again. The beatings from pure rage from my mother! I never understood her rage towards me. The teasing of me in public from my father! Their arguments that always seemed to include my name, but left me confused as to why.

You see, I had found my adoptive mother again after thirty years, for which I am grateful. This was when I was in therapy with my first EMDR therapist. They were the last years of her life. She was no longer filled with rage. She too, did not get what she deserved in her divorce and struggled throughout her life. But I was glad she found peace and a nice place to live with little money for the elderly. We never really talked about how severely she abused me, but she did her best to apologize. I would come to learn that she spent years volunteering in a shelter for domestic abuse victims. Women and children. Maybe that was her penance; who knows? I give her credit for treating me kindly and always welcoming me, the times I went to see her. But there was always one thing.

It was a look she would give me, along with an energy that I wouldn't truly understand until the end. It completed the puzzle a few years after her death.

It was a look like, "Did I figure it out yet ?" Me, Arden Ray. A look that included fear from her. I figured out that look of fear wasn't because of me possibly trying to kill her again. It was fear of knowledge. There were questions she refused to answer by changing the subject. There was the look she had once when I wore a pink button-down shirt along with, "I hate the color pink" and mumbled so I couldn't hear her.

There was the comment made to me about still watching people in silence, as if I could see right through them, just like I did as a child. She would also comment on what a smart child I was too. Then there was the look she would have when she looked at a picture of my daughter and then replying: "Oh my goodness, she is absolutely stunningly beautiful just like you were at that age!" How she then commented on how people would always comment on what a beautiful child I was. That last comment made me say, "But you always told me how ugly I was and I believed that for most of my life." It was the look she gave me that I didn't understand in that moment but later I would. The look is that she knew I would put the pieces together.

My mother would die the day before I was to go see her again. She had been in the hospital, died of a massive heart attack, and went quickly. I wasn't sad. I was grateful I was sober and grateful she did the best she could at the end of her life. I was surprised when the lady who came to help her once a week gave me this message. "It's okay that I didn't make it to the hospital in time to see my mother; she understood how difficult it was for me to go into a hospital to visit anyone." At that moment, I felt grateful that we ended on good terms with no guilt trips. It would turn out to be a puzzle piece, the only way she knew how to give me too. She knew I would figure it out and I feel she really wanted me to. Maybe that was part of her penance? I'm grateful not to be angry and that I have resolved issues with her. I hope she has found peace on the other side.

Those few months gave me answers even when I wasn't looking. I'd find myself in a situation and or a moment and think, "Well, no wonder." No wonder I don't like Squirt soda. No wonder I do not like anything cherry flavored. No wonder I can't stand cantaloupe and honey dew melon. No wonder I despise Nyquil and Vicks 44 cough syrup. No wonder I cannot stand the smell of Old Spice cologne and no wonder I drank. No wonder I dabbled in drugs and no wonder I married the men I did and stayed with my children's father as long as I did.

No wonder unconscious trauma can trigger unwanted choices. So many "NO WONDERS" but I was able to get through them, slowly, and move on.

Then one night it happened, I had the following dream....

There was a woman holding a little girl's hand, walking down a hallway with four doors. Two on each side, and at the end of the hallway was a bright light that shown through an archway. As the woman and little girl walked hand and hand, towards the archway, they looked into each opened door that had rooms full of light and flowers. One room had red roses, one room had sunflowers, one room had lilacs, and the last room had daffodils. When the two of them got to the end of the hallway, the woman got on her knees to hug the little girl. There were no words but there was love. There was no sadness, just peace. The woman stands up and the little girl gives a little wave with a smile as she walks into the bright light. Then the woman looks back at the hallway with its opened doors, and then turns and walks into the light. I woke up at that moment, thinking about that beautiful dream and found myself with unexpected happy tears.

For years, I had nightmares about a scared little girl running down a dark hallway, trying to get into any door. But the doors were all locked so she ran to the end of the hallway towards a light but there was a heavy iron gate and it was too heavy for her to lift. I always woke up scared and most times in another room because sleepwalking plagued me for years. But not that night.

I was finally free, and I felt it deep down in my heart and soul.

I have survived a lot.

More than a lot.

There are more things that I didn't include in this book, but I have cleared with therapy.

Wizard of Oz

I loved *The Wizard Of Oz* movie as a kid. I had watched it when I was young in the reflection of the living room windows at the lake house, while standing in the corner the entire time as a punishment.

When I would spill water on my mother, she never melted.

Then when I was stationed on Coronado in the Navy, I discovered the book was written right there, using the Hotel Del Coronado and a few other places on the island for L. Frank Baums' imagination. That movie has stuck with me my entire life. Now, I see the numerous metaphors as an adult and love it even more. The answers were right there all along; I just had to get on the right path, be brave, and keep moving forward. I have always had three Glenda's since my childhood. I did have strangers who tried to help me. People have things they hide by being scary and controlling. My little dog and longtime companion Rufus helped me along my way. But most of all, I learned that I could forgive. That forgiveness is sometimes hard and takes time.

I can forgive my first husband, who died a few years

ago from complications of alcoholism. He died never resolving the trauma he lived through in Vietnam. I truly hope he found the peace he needed on the other side.

I can forgive my second husband because he has unresolved issues and is not a happy man. I can be grateful he gave me two wonderful human beings that he loved and provided for.

I can even forgive Linda, the first EMDR therapist. Perhaps she got greedy with another client, and thus that was the reason she had to move out of town.

I can also forgive Alice, my biological mother. Turned out that she met me for her own selfish reasons, which I ended after a brief time getting to know her. Her feeling is that I am HER secret and shame that SHE has to live with, not me. She's a retired school teacher in Swansboro, North Carolina. The town she grew up in.

I can forgive my adoptive father, Bill (and that certainly took time) a very sick man. I don't mind that he was married to my stepmother, and they made each other miserable for over thirty years. I can forgive her too. My stepmother was an old woman in her 90's when she died, who never knew who she was, and lived in denial about what her husband did to her granddaughter.

So you see Virginia, that precious little baby you handed over to the wolves survived! The one good thing you did for me was the foster home you put me in when I was a day old. That couple, Elsie and Robert loved me. I know it in my heart. Their love for me was strong enough to carry me all these years. I truly believe that is why I did not become a psychopath. Why I have empathy and why I never abused my children nor used my tone with them.

I had all the right ingredients to wind up in prison like so many like me do. I know I am protected by angels. I know in my heart that voice I heard when my hands were around my mother's neck in full on rage, was that of my angel of protection.

Virginia, I hope when you read this, you will reconsider giving children to families with degrees and money, check their background, and give them to the people who will love and cherish them. To people who will give them a sturdy foundation that never rocks or cracks when they go out into the world.

Virginia, children do not have a voice, so it's your job to protect them by not falling for any facades.

Yes, Virginia I can even forgive you. The past is the past and even though I still have some blanks in my memory, I do not live there anymore. For I am the author of my own peace.

THE END

www.ingramcontent.com/pod-product-compliance
Lightning Source LLC
LaVergne TN
LVHW052024080426
835513LV00018B/2151